FIGHTERS over France
and the Low Countries

Bartłomiej Belcarz
Peter Taghon
Jean-Luis Roba
Robert Michulec
Jiri Railich
Roger Wallsgrove

Original concept by
Bartłomiej Belcarz

STRATUS

Published in Poland in 2002 by STRATUS
Artur Juszczak, Po. Box 123, 27-600 Sandomierz 1, Poland
e-mail: arturj@tarnobrzeg.tpnet.pl
for
Mushroom Model Publications,
36 Ver Road, Redbourn,
AL3 7PE, UK.
e-mail: rogerw@waitrose.com

© 2002 Mushroom Model Publications.

All rights reserved. Apart from any fair dealing for the purpose of private study, research, criticism or review, as permitted under the Copyright, Design and Patents Act, 1988, no part of this publication may be reproduced, stored in a retrieval system, or transmitted in any form or by any means, electronic, electrical, chemical, mechanical, optical, photocopying, recording or otherwise, without prior written permission. All enquiries should be addressed to the publisher.

ISBN 83-916327-1-7

Editor in chief	Roger Wallsgrove
Editors	Bartłomiej Belcarz
	Robert Pęczkowski
	Artur Juszczak
Edited by	Robert Pęczkowski
Page design by	Artur Juszczak
	Robert Pęczkowski
Cover Layout	Artur Juszczak
DTP	Robert Pęczkowski
	Artur Juszczak
Translation	Wojtek Matusiak
Proofreading	Roger Wallsgrove
Colour Drawings	Artur Juszczak
Photos	Bartłomiej Belcarz
	Peter Taghon
	Jean-Luis Roba
	Robert Michulec
	Jiri Railich
	Tomasz J. Kopański
	Robert Pęczkowski
	Wojtek Matusiak
	SHAA
	PI&SM
	CAW

Printed by:
Drukarnia Diecezjalna Sandomierz
ul. Żeromskiego 4,
27-600 Sandomierz
phone: +48 15 832 31 92

PRINTED IN POLAND

Table of contents

Introduction	3
The "Nederlandse Militaire Luchtvaart" in May 1940	5
The Belgian "Aéronautique Militaire" during the May-June 1940 campaign	19
RAF Fighters in France 1939-40	37
L'Armée de l'Air in the 1940 campaign	49
Jagdwaffe in France	75
Polish Air Force Fighters in France	97
Czech Fighters in France 1940	111
Colour Wartime Photos	129
Colour Profiles	135

War operations on the Western Front during May and June 1940 ran according to one scenario, the German one. The actual threat turned out to be far greater than the Allies had expected, and proved once more that the Second World War would not match their concepts of warfare.

The present work is intended to provide an overview of the French campaign of 1940. We have invited well-known authors to present the operations of that period as seen from the individual participating countries. Perhaps we will partly fill the gap there is, regarding the air war over Belgium, Holland, Luxembourg, and France in May and June 1940.

Bartłomiej Belcarz

Donation of the eight MS 406 to Escadrille "France" by gen. Nollet president of La Caisse Autonome de la Defence Nationale. 17 June 1939.

T. Kopański coll.

Jean-Louis Roba

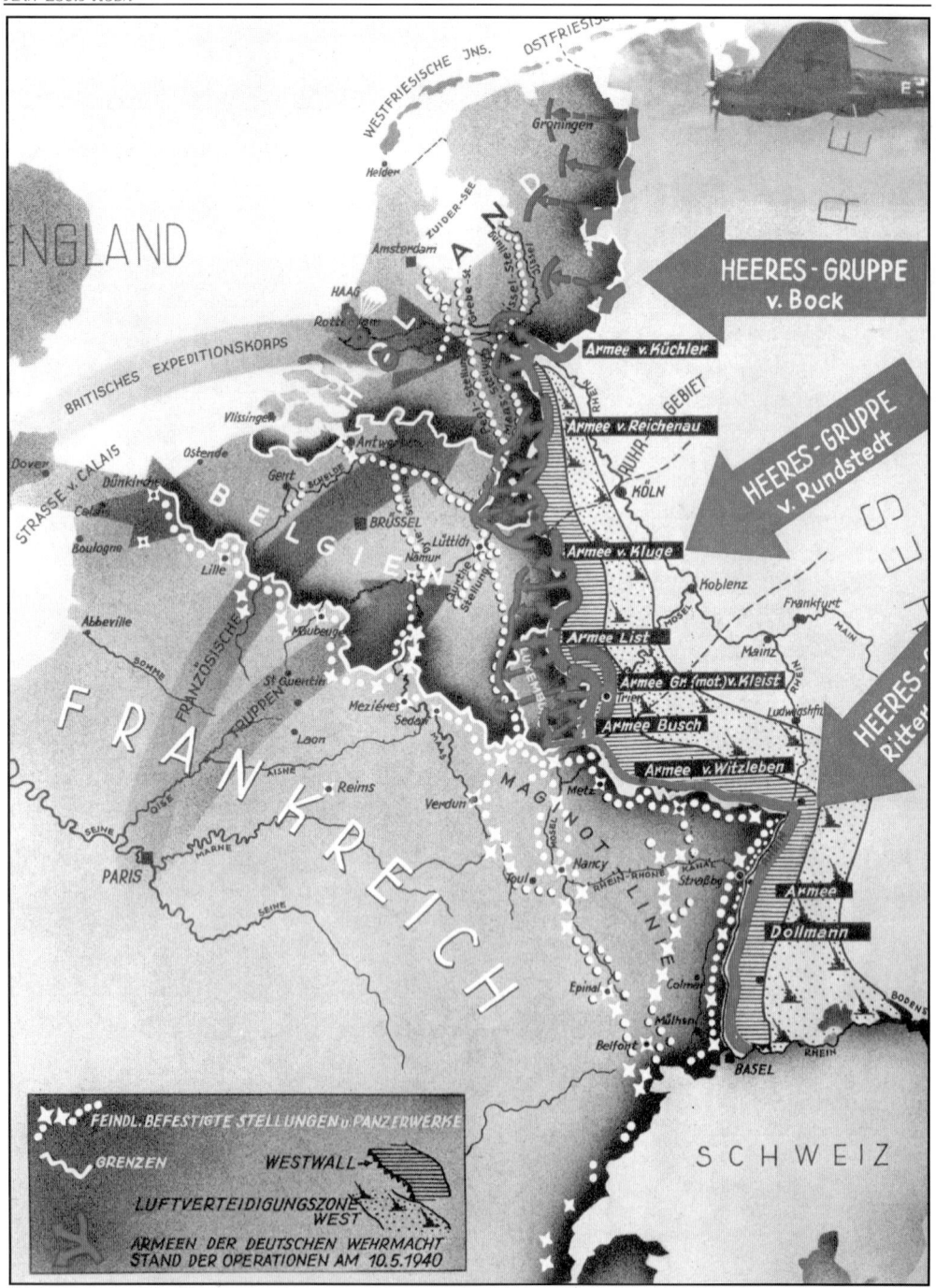

Map of German attack on Low Countries.
Map was originally published in "Wehrmachtberichte Weltgeschichte, Der Krieg 1939/40" by Verlag Die Wehrmacht K. G., Berlin, 1941

4 Fighters ...

The "Nederlandse Militaire Luchtvaart" in May 1940
by Jean-Louis Roba

In the period of the "Phoney War", the Netherlands experienced some aerial incidents. Contrary to some other neutral countries, the Dutch Government decided to actively defend its airspace, in spite of the weakness of its airforce. That decision was reinforced after the first (and dangerous) interceptions were launched.

A serious incident for the Militaire Luchtvaart occurred on 13th September 1939, when a Do 18 flying boat attacked, by mistake, a Fokker T.VIII floatplane, forced it to land and, landing itself on the sea, captured the entire crew (who were soon freed, with German Government apologies). The same day, another Do 18 of 2./106 severely damaged by Dutch fighters was captured, its crew being interned. On 18th January 1940, a Blohm & Voss flying boat was intercepted and damaged. On 28th March, a Whitley of 77 Sqn RAF was shot down while, on 14th April, a Blenheim of 57 Sqn RAF suffered the same fate. Other planes of both sides crashed on Dutch soil but without intervention of the local airforce. Notice that civilian planes were not spared. A serious incident occurred on 26th September 1939 when the DC-3 PH-ASM "Mees" of KLM, arriving from Sweden, was machine-gunned by a patrolling He 115. A Swedish passenger was killed, but the DC-3 managed to land at Schiphol.

On the eve of the German invasion, the most effective units of the Netherlands Airforce (Nederlandse Militaire Luchtvaart) were organised in two flying regiments (or Luchtvaartregimenten):

Douglas 8-A n° 391 was destroyed during the German raid on Ockenburg airfield. In the background we can see no. 396.
P. Thagon coll.

1st Regiment:
– 1st Group:
a reconnaissance squadron (Strategische Verkennings Afdeling):
10 Fokker C.X, (Bergen).
a bomber squadron (Bombardier Vliegtuig Afdeling):
9 Fokker T.V, (Schiphol).
– 2nd Group (fighters tasked with the defence of the territory):
1st fighter squadron (1e Ja.V.A.=Jachtvliegtuig Afdeling):
11 Fokker D.XXI (De Kooy).
2nd fighter squadron (2e Ja.V.A.): 9 Fokker D.XXI (Schiphol).
3rd fighter squadron (3e Ja.V.A.): 11 Fokker G.1A (Waalhaven).
4th fighter squadron (4e Ja.V.A.): 12 Fokker G.1A (Bergen).
2nd Regiment (mainly involved in Army co-operation):
– 1st recce Group (Verkennings Groep):
1 Fokker C.X, 4 Fokker C.V and 4 Koolhoven FK-51 (Hilversum).
– 2nd recce Group:
7 Fokker C.V and 5 Koolhoven FK-51 (Ypenburg).
– 3rd recce Group:
9 Fokker C.V and 4 Koolhoven FK-51 (Ruigenhoek).
– 4th recce Group:
7 Fokker C.V and 3 Koolhoven FK-51 (Gilze-Rijen).
– Fighter Group attached to the Army (Jachtgroep veldleger):
1st squadron: 8 Fokker-D.XXI (Ypenburg).
3rd squadron: 11 Douglas 8-A (Ypenburg).
Alongside those fighting units, we must mention:
– 76 training planes used in Flying Schools (Fokker S.IV and S.IX, C.V) (Vlissingen, Haamstede, Texel);

Another Douglas 8 at Ockenburg, here no. 397.
P. Thagon coll.

6 *Fighters ...*

Ju 52 and burned out Douglas 8 at Ockenburg.
P. Thagon coll.

– 56 planes dispersed on some airfields (and mainly used as hacks or second line machines) with no great military value;
– 53 floatplanes of the Navy (Marine Luchtvaart Dienst), mainly Fokkers (C.VII, C.VIII, C.XIV and T.VIII) (De Mok, de Kooy, Schellinwoude).

To support its invasion of the Netherlands, the Luftwaffe assembled:
– II. and III./JG 26 (and the subordinated III./JG 3):
equipped with Bf 109;
– I./JG 51 (and subordinated groups: I./JG 20, I./JG 26 and II./JG 27): equipped with Bf 109;
– II./Trägergruppe 186: equipped with Bf 109;
– I. and II./ZG 26: equipped with Bf 110;
– I., II. and III./KG 4: equipped with He 111;
– I./KGr.126: equipped with He 111;
– I./KG 30: equipped with Ju 88;
– IV./LG 1: equipped with Ju 87;
– 7./LG 2: recce unit equipped with Do 17;
– Seefliegergruppe: equipped with He 115 floatplanes;
– Staffel Schwilden: equipped with He 59 floatplanes;
– I., II., III. and IV./KGzbV 1: transport unit equipped with Ju 52;
– I., II. and III./KGzbV 2: transport unit equipped with Ju 52;
– 4.(H)/21 and 4.(H)/23: equipped with Hs 126 (army cooperation).

The most prominent day in the invasion was naturally 10th May. The German Airforce had two tasks:
– To capture strategic points using airborne troops (paratroopers and infantrymen of 22nd Infantry Divisionloaded in transports or floatplanes);

German Flak at Waalhaven. In the background we see Fokker G-1A no. 302

A German soldier seeks shelter in a Dutch blockhouse. In the background we see what remains of Fokker G1.A no. 302 after the explosion of a bomb.
P. Thagon coll.

– To destroy Dutch airfields to annihilate the local airforce and prevent the arrival of RAF or French Arméede l'Air reinforcements.

At Amsterdam-Schiphol, around 6.00 H (German time), Fokker D.XXIs took off to intercept German bombers (identified as Ju 88s); no claims were made but, when the bombs fell, eight Fokker T.Vs took off and claimed three planes shot down and three more damaged.

Waalhaven was the target of the He 111s of KG 4. The leading aircraft of the German formation was attacked by two Fokker G.1A of 3e Ja.V.A (3rd squadron) and shot down. Its observer was Oberst Martin Fiebig, KG 4's Kommodore! This high-ranked officer was captured with the three other crewmen (Fiebig was freed after the fall of Netherlands, becoming a general who would later serve in the Mediterranean area). Two other bombers of

Troops of 22. Luftlandedivision prepare for take off in their Ju 52.
P. Thagon coll.

8 Fighters ...

A Fokker T.V. of Bom.VA left behind at Schiphol airfield.
P. Thagon coll.

5/KG 4 were shot down by the Fokkers but the Dutch planes were severely damaged by return fire and had to land at Waalhaven where they would be soon captured. On the airfield, damage was heavy. Three planes were destroyed on the ground and the hangars and military installations were set on fire.

The six surviving Fokkers, having taken off, shot down three Ju 88s of I./KG 30 attacking Dutch AA guns to protect the arrival of the transport fleet. Indeed, Ju 52 of KGzbV 1 flew to that area loaded with paratroopers of FJR 1 (1st paratrooper regiment) and soldiers of I.R. 16 (the 16th infantry regiment, part of 22nd infantry division) having as targets the town of Rotterdam, its airfields and the bridges over the River Meuse (Maas) (C.O.

Hptm. Robitzsch, Staffelkapitän of 5./TrGr 186 in his Bf 109 E-4 «Der Alte» preparing to take off
J. L. Roba coll.

The Bf 109 E-4 of Hptm. Robitzsch of 5./TrGr 186 after his crash-landing on De Kooy Airfield. Hptm. Robitzsch was shot down by Lt. van Overvest on 10th May.
J. L. Roba coll.

of that operation was the famed General Kurt Student). The transport planes were protected by Bf 109s (two of them claimed by the Dutch fighters).

A Fokker was destroyed and the five surviving planes (some of them having strafed the landed Ju52s unloading their men in Rotterdam area) had to find shelter on other bases. Indeed, Waalhaven would again be bombed by KG 4 and soon overrun by German airborne troops.

At Bergen, airbase of 4e Ja.V.A., the units were surprised on the ground by the German bombers. Nearly all the planes were destroyed or damaged. A lone Fokker D.XXI took off but, outclassed in the air, came back without any claim.

At De Kooy, eleven Fokker D.XXIs of 1e Ja.V.A. met He 111s and Ju 88s. A claim was made but a Dutch fighter was lost in the concentrated defensive fire of three He 111s.

At Ypenburg, eight Fokker D.XXIs and eleven Douglas 8-As took off before the bombs fell on the airfield, causing much damage and destroying two planes. The Dutch fighters did not attack the bombers but met the second transport fleet (tasked to secure the three airfields in the vicinity of the Dutch capital - Ypenburg, Ockenburg and Valkenburg - then to enter The Hague and capture the Government, an operation under the command of General Hans Graf von Sponeck, C.O. of 22nd Infantry Division). The Dutch fighters claimed at least one Ju52 but suffered some losses from the escorting Bf 110s.

Another view of the Bf 109 E-4 of Hptm. Robitzsch on De Kooy airfield.
J. L. Roba coll.

Douglas 8 A3N No. 392, the plane of Sgts. Kuhn and Staal of 3e Ja.V.A., pictured during the Phoney War at Ypenburg. This plane was shot down on the 10th of May in combat with a Bf 110 and crashed at Zoetermeer.
J. L. Roba coll.

Four of them had to land on airfields already captured by the airborne troops and only one plane of 1e Ja.V.A. escaped. The Douglases also claimed a Ju 52, but all were shot down by the escorting Zerstörers or had to land in a hurry, being destroyed or put out of use. In the first hours of 10th May, the Ypenburg units were annihilated.

When the German second wave attacked, the remnants of Militaire Luchtvaart tried to concentrate their actions. From Ruigenhoek, four D.XXIs of 2e Ja.V.A., reinforced by the survivor from Ypenburg, claimed a Ju 52 but a Dutch plane was shot down by a Bf 109.

At De Kooy, an important dogfight took place between eight D.XXIs of 1e Ja.V.A. and Bf 109s of II./Tr.Gr.186. The Dutch claimed five enemy fighters while the Germans claimed seven or eight Fokkers! In fact, the German pilots were totally surprised by the slow speed of the D.XXI and

Ju 52s that landed on the Rijksweg between Delft and Rotterdam were shot up by G. 1As 322 and 303 during the afternoon of the 11th May. Here, some refugee civilians inspect the planes.
J. L. Roba coll.

A formation of Fokker C.Xs of Strat. Ver. V.A. based at Bergen airfield, during a training flight during the Phoney War. The C.X 713 saw action on the 13th May, when 4 C.Xs bombed and shot up German troops at Grebbeberg.
Schuurman coll.

could not accurately target them. Two Bf 109s were shot down by the manoeuverable Dutch fighters. One pilot was killed, the other one, the 5./186 Staffelkapitän Hptm Dieter Robitzsch, was captured. He did not have the luck of KG 4's Kommodore. Indeed, Robitzsch was transferred to a British unit and evacuated to England. He ended the war in Canada. One Fokker was destroyed on landing and the seven others were severely damaged. When they were repaired, a second German attack destroyed three of them.

In the latter part of the morning, all available Dutch planes were sent to bomb the German landing areas. Nearly all those bombing missions were

A burned out Fokker C.X of Strat. Ver. V.A. at Bergen airfield.
Schuurman coll.

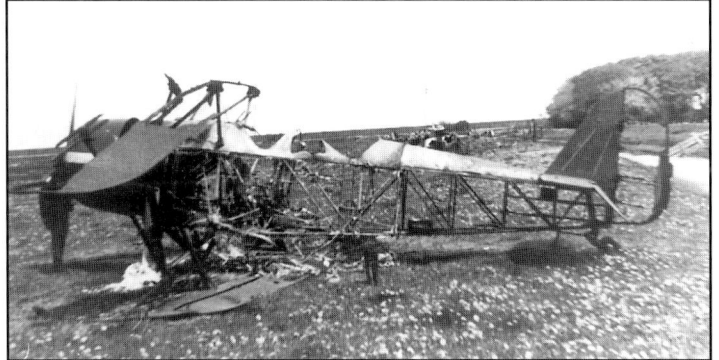

A burned out Koolhoven FK-51 on De Kooy airfield.
J. L. Roba coll.

made without fighter escort, as there were insufficient planes. Some Ju 52s were destroyed or heavily damaged on the ground by bombs, but it is naturally impossible to give their numbers as there was, as so often, overclaiming. Today it is impossible to distinguish the losses of transport planes caused by bad landings, Dutch AA, or bombs.

Near Waalhaven, two Fokker C.Xs had to belly-land after being attacked by Bf 109s. Coming back from bombing Ockenburg, four Fokker T.Vs met Bf 109s and one Dutch plane was shot down over North Sea. Later, another plane was severely damaged by Dutch AA.

Many of the airfields around Rotterdam and The Hague having been overrun by the Germans, the few available planes of Militaire Luchtvaart evacuated to other landing grounds: such as Noordwijkenhout and Middenmeer.

Another nice view of a Fokker C.X of Strat. Ver. V.A. during the Phoney War.
Schuurman coll.

*Fighters ... **13***

Another view of the destroyed Ju 52s along the highway between Delft and Rotterdam.
P. Thagon coll.

The reconnaissance Fokker C.Vs were equipped with bombs and were requested to attack too the concentrations of grounded Ju 52s. Between Haamstede and Waalhaven, two C.Vs of 4th Group were intercepted by Bf 109s. One was shot down and the second crash landed, being destroyed by the explosion of its own bombs.

The sole bombing action protected by fighters was launched around 5 p.m. when six Fokker D.XXIs of 2e Ja.V.A. escorted three Fokker T.Vs from Schiphol. One fighter and two bombers were lost to Bf 109s on the way back. A second D.XXI was severely damaged. One Bf 109 was claimed.

The Dutch seaplanes were active too that 10th May. A Fokker T.VIII took off in the morning for a coastal reconnaissance but was attacked by a Bf 110 when coming back to Lake Braasemermeer. Dutch AA shot down or damaged the intruder. Later four T.VIIIs started for The Hague to load members of the Dutch Government. Three were intercepted by German fighters and two of the seaplanes destroyed (the third could be repaired). Only one seaplane reached England with two Ministers on board. A Fokker C.XIV, engaged in the Petten area, claims to have shot down an attacking Bf 109.

Wrecked Fokker G-1 at Waalhaven.
Botquin coll.

Another view of the destroyed Fokker G-1 at Waalhaven.
Botquin coll.

At the end of 10th May, the German goals were attained. Two large airborne forces had landed near two important Dutch cities and strategic points (such as bridges). The Luftwaffe suffered some losses but Militair Luchtvaart was decimated, being no longer able to hinder the operations over the Low Countries. If we have mentioned the actions of Dutchplanes, we must not neglect the good AA defence. For instance, that day Lt Wolfgang Ludewig's Bf 109 of9./JG 26 was hit by ground fire when trying to land at Ypenburg to reconnoitre his own positions. Captured by Dutch troops, the pilot would be soon freed. Many Ju 52s too were victims of the accurate AA fire and all German aerial losses in the Netherlands should not to be attributed to the actions of the Dutch fighters.

The main effort having been accomplished the day before, on 11th May, III./JG 3 was retired from the areato operate over Belgium. JG 26 continued to fly over the Netherlands but fought mainly that day over the

Destroyed hangar of Dutch seaplanes.
　　　　R. Pęczkowski coll.

Belgian/Dutch borders with French fighters. But a part of KG 54 (equipped with He 111s) operating before over Belgium/France was called to bomb specific targets in Southern Holland (KG 54 would come back over the Netherlands three days later). On the other side, the Dutch Airforce tried to find reinforcements.

Damaged planes were repaired in the night. Six obsolete Fokker D.XVIIs were recalled from De Vlijt flying school. The Fokker factory at Schiphol helped repair some fighters.

Some patrols were launched by the remaining fighters and Ju 52s were claimed in the air or on the ground. Indeed, these three-engined transport planes made shuttle runs to bring men and munitions to the airborne troops still fighting around Rotterdam or near the Meuse (Maas) bridges. The most aggressive action in the morning was an attack by three Fokker T.V bombers against those bridges near Rotterdam. Escorted by three D.XXIs, the bombers missed their target. They came back over the bridges later in the afternoon but, at that time, had to fight against Bf 110s. Some of the latter were claimed by the Dutch, who lost nevertheless one T.V and one fighter. A second D.XXI, hit by "friendly" AA, was abandoned by its pilot.

In fact, Dutch AA proved to be very dangerous firing against all planes. A Bf 109 of 6./Tr.Gr.186 was hit north of Den Helder and crash-landed, the pilot (Uffz. Werner Haase) becoming POW. The Kapitän of 5./JG26, Oblt. Hubertus von Holtey, was also a victim of AA guns south of Zuiderzee, becoming POW too (he was freed after the fall of the Netherlands). Lt. Lothar Scheffler of 4./JG 27 was hit near Tiel and crash-landed (sent to England, he did not return to his unit at the end of the campaign). But that day, a Fokker D.XVII and a C.V were also shot down by Dutch ground fire.

German bombers launched new attacks against every military target (columns on the roads or defensive positions) and bombed the remaining airfields still in Dutch hands, destroying installations and, at least two

C.Vs (and two C.XIV seaplanes at De Mok). As mentioned before, on 11th May German fighters encountered planes of the French Armée de l'Air and British RAF (those last ones mainly in coastal areas). Dog-fighting became more aggressive.

If 11th May was relatively "quiet" for the Militair Luchtvaart, the Dutch Airforce came back in force on 12th May. Thanks to their mechanics, the Dutch could still fight, with around fifty serviceable planes.

It was no longer possible to defend Dutch airspace. The Dutch flyers could only hope to destroy as many enemy planes as possible, attack German columns, and support the Allied airforces. In the morning, two sections of two C.Xs escorted by six D.XXIs dropped bombs on concentrations of landed Ju 52s.

Two attacks were launched with a handful of planes against advancing German columns in the Wageningen area. Three G.1.As were severely damaged by Flak protecting the advance, and a C.V was shot down. C.Vs of 3rd Group launched eleven bombardment operations in area Delft-Rotterdam, on Frisian and – again –Wageningen, but naturally only with a small number of planes. Two of them were shot down by Bf 109s (probably of 4./JG 27) and one by Flak (a fourth one being damaged too by Flak). Dutch AA guns were still very accurate. Uffz. Günther Feld of 6./Tr.Gr.186 was shot down north of Den Helder and captured.

On 13th May, at dawn, the Militair Luchtvaart tried to attack Moerdijk bridge with very limited forces: a sole T.V (from the annihilated Bom.V.A.), escorted by two Fokker G.1.As! The bombs missed the target and, on the way back, the Dutch were intercepted by 4./JG 26. The bomber and a fighter were credited to Hptm. Karl Ebbinghausen, the Staffelkapitän.

Two mixed patrols, with five D.XXIs, two G.1.As and four C.Xs, strafed German columns. One Bf 109 was claimed but one G.1.A had to be

Destroyed Fokker XX.
R. Pęczkowski coll.

Fighters ... 17

German soldier in Dutch aircraft cockpit.
R. Pęczkowski coll.

abandoned. That day, the Fokker company delivered three G.1.Bs initially designed to be sold to Finland. They came nevertheless too late.

Indeed, 14th May would be the last day of fighting for the Militair Luchtvaart. The number of its planes was severely reduced, most of them being damaged and suffering too from lack of ammunition. They had to move regularly to avoid being bombed on their airfields. In spite of its total weakness, the Dutch Airforce tried to mount a few missions against all odds. Five Fokker G.1s (somerepaired in hurry during the preceding night) of 4e Ja.V.A. set off in the morning with five D.XXIs to strafe German troops. One G.1 was damaged when taking off and a D.XXI was shot down by "friendly" fire. In the afternoon, two Fokker C.Xs launched reconnaissance missions near Rotterdam and Doordrecht, but oneof them failed in the face of enemy air superiority. The last mission must have been two C.Vs trying to reconnoitre some positions west of Utrecht.

On 14th May, the Netherlands sued for peace but, nevertheless, following a misinterpretation of orders, Rotterdam was attacked by bombers of KG 54, the town being partly destroyed by fire (General Student himself was seriously wounded). Some sources soon mentioned for propaganda purposes that the bombing caused the death of 30,000 civilians but, in fact, casualties were not so high and are estimated as between 600 and 900.

Seeing that "the game is over", some Dutch planes escaped that day to Belgium and/or France. For example, on the night of 13th/14th May, all remaining seaplanes receive the order to fly to Boulogne-sur-Mer and later to Brest before going on to England (the Fokker T.VIIIs joined the new 320 (Dutch) squadron). The planes which could not be evacuated were blown up by the Dutch crews and mechanics. The armistice became official on 15th May in the morning.

The Belgian "Aéronautique Militaire" during the May-June 1940 campaign.
by Peter Taghon

During the night of the 9th/10th of May, the Belgian Government received a message from its military attaché in Berlin that the German attack in the West was to be launched next morning. The Army and the Aéronautique Militaire were immediately alerted and sent to their campaign bases.

Early in the morning, when the first Luftwaffe planes entered Belgian airspace, the movement of the squadrons was not yet completed. At Schaffen/Diest airfield there was a discussion between Capt. Charlier, the Commander of the Hurricane Sqn., and Lt. Van den Hove. There was fog, and Lt. Van den Hove proposed to wait until the sun broke through. The Hurricanes of 2./I./2. Aé, the Gloster Gladiators of 1./I./2. Aé. and the Fairey Foxes of 7./III./3. Aé. were already on the runway as a formation of Dornier Do17s of KG 77 appeared. The airfield was bombed with SC 50 bombs and raked with small arms fire. The Glosters of Capt. Guisgand were just taking-off, and two were destroyed. The Hurricanes suffered heavier losses, only Capt. Van den Hove and Corp. Jacobs reaching Le Culot airfield. During that flight Capt. Van den Hove sighted a formation of He 111s (probably KG 27) and attacked. The last He 111 left the formation, it was the first "probable" victory of the Aé. Militaire. At Schaffen, all 7 Foxes of 7./III./3. Aé. were burning. The Dorniers then continued on their way to raid Goetsenhoven airfield, where most of the Foxes and Koolhovens of 4 School Sqn. were destroyed.

Battle T.63 and T.71 during a training flight in the spring of 1940.
P. Taghon coll.

Map of German advance on 11 May 1940.
Map was originally published in "Wehrmachtberichte Weltgeschichte, Der Krieg 1939/40" by Verlag Die Wehrmacht K. G., Berlin, 1941

Aéronautique Militaire

One of the Fairey Battles of 5./III./3. Aé. destroyed during the bombing of Aalter airfield on the 18th May.

P. Taghon coll.

II./2. Aé. on Nivelles airfield was luckier. The take-off of the Fiat CR 42s was also delayed, but as a Staffel of Ju 87s of StG 2 bombed the airfield, most of the planes were already on their way to Brustem. During the flight, Capt. de Callatay attacked a Ju 52 of 17./KGzbV 5 and shot it down. Some time later five Fiats took off to protect Brustem airfield. They intercepted two Do 17s, and one of the bombers was damaged by Lt. Offenberg. 1/Sgt. Maes scored a probable on the second one. During the interception the Fiats were attacked by Bf 109s of JG 1. 1/Sgt Delanny's Fiat was lost, the pilot killed. During that dogfight, Lt. Goffin damaged a Bf 109, the pilot, Oblt. Dutel, reaching Achen where he crash-landed. At about 08.25 h in the morning a Fiat platoon took off to protect a reconnaissance mission by a Renard R.31 of V./1. Aé. in de Hasselt-Maaseik region. They met no German planes and returned safely to Brustem.

Nivelles, spring 1940; Sgt. Van Molkot, Capt. Jean de Callatay and Corp. Hansel pose near one of the newly arrived Fiat CR 42.

P. Taghon coll.

Fighters ... 21

Lt. Offenberg, scored at least one victory on the Fiat CR 42.
P. Taghon coll.

In the meantime Evere airfield was attacked by small formations of He 111s of KG 27. All of the Battles escaped and landed at Belsele. A "Kette" of He 111s of KG 27 followed the fleeing Battles and bombed Belsele airfield. When the attackers turn away, one of the Battles was burning. The Battle-Group under Major Piot then moved to Aalter airfield. The Foxes of I./3.Aé. were able to evacuate Evere and land in Neerhespen, only to be bombed by the Dornier Do 17s of KG 77. They suffered heavy losses.

The Foxes of 5. and 6./III./2. Aé. evacuated to Vissenaken airfield. At 08.35 h three platoons took off to attack a formation of He 111s. They were soon engaged by a large formation of Bf 109s of I./JG 27. Although the biplane fighters were no match for the Messerschmitts, Lt. Dufossez managed to shoot down the Bf 109 of Fw. Hoppe. He was then surprised by another Bf 109 and had to abandon his aircraft, O-123. His parachute was damaged and he fell to his death. A second Fox, O-127 of 1/Sgt. Detal, was also shot down, but this pilot survived. After the dogfight, a few Foxes continued to protect the airspace. They were soon engaged by the Bf 109s of I/JG 21. O-111 of Lt. Brel was lost, the pilot killed. Three more Foxes returned badly damaged to Vissenaken. At 11.00 h a platoon Foxes of 6./III./2. Aé. was charged to protect a reconnaissance mission by a Fox of III./1. Aé. (Sgt. Potelle/Lt. Leonard) in the Verviers area. They met no enemy opposition.

Almost all the reconnaissance planes of 1. Aé (Fairey Foxes and Renard R.31s) were able to join their wartime bases and made a total of 7 missions during the day. The Fox of Lt. Malchair was shot down by Flak near Eupen. The crew returned.

At noon, three Fiats took off to protect a Renard R.31 of VI./1. Aé. (Sgt. Rigolle/S/Lt. Walch) above the Albert Canal. On the way back, Lt. Prince de

The R.26 of 1/Sgt. Jean Maes after the bombing of Chartres airfield.
P. Taghon coll.

22 Fighters ...

Fairey Fox of 7./1. Aé. at its base in Goetsenhoven. Note the overall olive colour.
        P. Taghon coll.

Merode attacked and claimed a Do 17, probably a plane of 2(F)/123 (Oblt. von Schaessler) which crash-landed at Mönchen-Gladbach. In the meantime Brustem airfield was attacked by a Staffel of Bf 109s. Two Fiats were shot up. Shortly afterwards, Brustem was attacked by the Ju 87s of I./StG 2. 14 Fiats of 3./II./2. Aé. were destroyed. Vissenaken was also raided and 4 more Foxes of I./3. Aé. were set on fire.

At the end of the day, the Aéronautique Militaire had lost a total of 80 planes, or about 45% of its initial strength, 39 of them fighters.

During the 11th the Aé. Militaire gave orders to attack the bridges over the Albert Canal. Three platoons of Fairey Battles of III./3. Aé. were detailed, one to each of the three bridges. For their protection, two platoons of Gloster Gladiators of 1./I./2. Aé. operated from 06.00 h onwards over the Albert Canal. Due to problems with their bomb load, the Battles took off too late. Meanwhile, the Gloster Gladiators were intercepted by a formation Bf 109s of I./JG 1. In a wild dogfight 4 of the 6 biplanes were shot down. 1/Sgt. Rolin claimed a Bf 109, only to be downed by another Messerschmitt. He escaped from his plane and became a POW. The Gladiator G-19 of Sgt. Pirlot was also lost, and the pilot remains to this day "missing in action". G-31 of Sgt. Vanden Broeck was damaged, but returned to base. The plane was a write off. The second platoon suffered a similar fate. Capt. Guisgand's plane was shot up and the Sqn/Ldr. made an emergency landing near Waremme. Sgt. Clinquart was killed when his G-34 crashed near Fexhe-Slins. Only Sgt. Winand was able to return to Beauvechain.

Fighters ... 23

Fairey Fox of 7./1. Aé. at its base in Goetsenhoven. Remark the overall olive colour.

P. Taghon coll.

As the Battles arrived in the target area, they had no protection at all. Aircraft T.60 (Adjt. Verbraeck/Adjt. Dôme) didn't even reach the target in Veldwezelt. The Battle was attacked by a He 111 and shot down near Lebbeke. The crew returned wounded to Aalter. Near Hasselt the two other Battles of the Veldwezelt platoon were attacked by the Bf 109s of 1/JG 27. T.58 (Adjt. Timmermans/1/Sgt. Rolin-Hymans) was downed by Oblt. Redlich, and the crew killed. So only Capt. Pierre/Lt. Cloquette bombed the bridge, but the 50 kg-bombs did no harm to the structure. T.73 returned damaged to Aalter. The platoon of Capt. Glorie attacked the bridge at Vroenhoven. The Battles met fierce flak and two of the planes, including T.70 of Capt. Glorie, were shot down. His observer, S/Lt. Vandenbosch, survived wounded. On board T.61 (Adjt. Delvigne/Sgt. Moens) there were no survivors. T. 64 (Adjt. Binon/Corp. Legand) returned damaged to base. The Briegden platoon lost quickly T.71 (Adjt. Vandevelde/Corp. Bergmans). The gunner was wounded by groundfire and the plane had to abort. T.62 (1/Adjt. Jordens/Sgt. de Ribeaucourt) was damaged by fire from Belgian troops and the crew had to take to their parachutes. The last Battle, T.68 (1/Sgt. Wieseler/Adjt. de Coninck), was shot down by flak and crash-landed near Herk de Stad.

Meanwhile, the Luftwaffe continued to bomb the Belgian airfields. The 8 surviving Fiats of II./2. Aé had just left Brustem as the airfield was raided. The planes escaped to Nieuwkerken-Waas. I./2. Aé. was not so lucky. At 14.00 h. Beauvechain airfield was straffed by I./JG 1, and seven Glosters were destroyed. At 16.30 h. the base was again attacked and as the Messerschmitts finished their work, all the remaining Glosters and Hurricanes were burning. At Vissenaken III./2. Aé. was raided by a Staffel of Ju 87s, and five Foxes were lost. The airfield was evacuated and the Group moved to Moerbeke. Ju 87s of StG 2 dive-bombed Neerhespen airfield, only one Fairey Fox of I./3. Aé. surviving. It was destroyed shortly afterwards, as

24 Fighters ...

Aéronautique Militaire

the base was evacuated. Jeneffe, base of III./1. Aé., was also strafed by Bf 109s. The 2 remaining Foxes and a Morane were left behind.

The other Squadrons of 1. Aé. continued their reconnaissance missions. A total of 8 sorties were flown. The Renard R.31 of Sgt. Boute/S/Lt. Berhaut was shot down and crash-landed in 's Herenelderen. By noon the crew returned to their base. Early in the morning, a Fairey Fox of II./1. Aé (Sgt. Bailly/Lt. Desmeth) made a recce flight over the Netherlands. The plane was protected by a platoon of Foxes of 5./III./2. Aé., and returned with valuable information to Glabbeek.

Above:
Fairey Fox O-178, a plane of 6./III./2. Aé., pictured at Vissenaken airfield on January 1940.
Below:
The remains of a Fairey Fox of III./ 1. Aé. at Jeneffe airfield.

Both photos
P. Taghon coll.

Fighters ... 25

Lt. Brel in O-111, pictured in the spring of 1940. He was killed on the 10th May, in a dogfight with Bf 109s of I./JG 21
P. Taghon coll.

Due to the heavy losses, the Aéronautique was reorganised on the 12th. All bombing missions were suspended. I./ 3. Aé, II./3. Aé., and I./2. Aé. were no longer operational and had to evacuate to France. III./2. Aé. delivered its remaining Foxes to II./ 2. Aé. before leaving the territory. The 8 Fiats of II./2. Aé. were kept on the ground and the only missions flown were reconnaissance flights. Two Foxes of 7/III./3. Aé. took off for the Namur-Huy area. O-175 (Adjt. Vos/Lt. Dulait) was damaged by groundfire and destroyed on landing. During another mission over Namur Fox O-187 (1/Sgt. Mot/Lt. Lefebvre) was shot down by a Morane of GC III./2. The crew survived and returned. Three of the remaining Battles also made a reconnaissance sortie. They met no Luftwaffe fighters and returned to Aalter.

On the 13th, six Fiat CR 42s of II./2. Aé flew two "missions d'interdiction" in the Leuven-Tienen-Westerlo area. They met no enemy opposition and returned safe to their base at Nieuwkerke. During the day the Foxes and Battles made a total of 11 reconnaissance missions. Seven crews were tasked

Most of the Fairey Foxes of I./ 3. Aé. were destroyed during the bombing of Neerhespen airfield by StG 2 on the 11th. The planes were poorly camouflaged and an easy target for the dive-bombers.
P. Taghon coll.

26 Fighters ...

Burnt-out Gloster Gladiator of 1./I/2. 2aé. at Beauvechain airfield. In two strafings during the afternoon of the 11th, the Bf109s of JG 1 destroyed all the remaining Glosters and Hurricanes of I./2.Aé.
P. Taghon coll.

to observe the German advance at the Maas-Scheldekanaal. None of these planes had a fighter escort. No enemy fighters were encountered, but two Foxes of III./2. Aé. were shot down by groundfire. The crews survived. A further Fox, O-169, was destroyed in a crash-landing at Belgrade, after a flight in the Namur area. This crew also returned to its unit. Meanwhile two more Groups, I./2. Aé. and III./3. Aé. , left Belgian soil and transferred to Norrent Fontes in France.

The following day, six Fiat CR 42s were tasked to protect the evacuation of 3. Corps in the Fleurus area. The planes took off at 11.13 h. under the command of Capt. Jean de Callatay. On the way to Fleurus, 1/Sgt. de Moerloze attacked a German bomber, but the plane escaped. Shortly afterwards, the five other Fiats were engaged by a formation of Bf 109s of 8./JG 3. Capt. de Callatay managed to get on the tail of one of the Messerschmitts, but soon had to break off the fight as he was pursued by another Bf 109. S/Lt. Papeians placed two bursts into a Bf 109, but his

One of the Gloster Gladiators of I./2. Aé. lost during the raid on Schaffen airfield on the 10th of May.
P. Taghon coll.

*Fighters ... **27***

Above:
Nice view of Gloster Gladiator G-23, pictured during the spring of 1940 at Schaffen-Diest.

Below:
Gloster Gladiator G-24 during a training flight in the spring of 1940

Both photos P. Taghon coll.

machine-guns jammed before he could finish off his foe. Adjt. Francois was shot down and made an emergency landing near Nivelles. The plane was a write-off, the pilot returned. After the dogfight, Capt. de Callatay and 1/Sgt. Michotte each claim a Bf 109. In fact 8/JG 3 lost no planes at all. The German records also show overclaiming - Oblt. Gäth, Fw. Bauer, Uffz. Saborowski and Uffz. Flebbe each claimed a Fiat.

Meanwhile, the Command of the Aéronautique Militaire ordered II./2.Aé to make a propaganda flight with the old Fairey Firefly. The pilots have to show the Belgian colours to the troops on the front. The formation took off at 15.20 h. Maj. Jacques Lamarche, Group commander and a veteran of the First World War, led. Near Keerbergen the Fireflies encountered heavy groundfire. The Belgian troops were not used to seeing allied planes and shot at anything that flew. The Firefly of Adjt. Leroy du Vivier was hit

28 *Fighters ...*

in the engine and the pilot made a crash-landing. He survived, slightly injured.

The other Squadrons of the Aéronautique Militaire made the usual reconnaissance flights. A total of 10 missions were flown, two by the Battles of 5./3. Aé., the others by a Fairey Fox and a Renard R.31 of 1. Aé. The two Fairey Battles returned damaged and were written off. One Fox (Adjt. de la Bastita/S/Lt. Remy) was shot down over the German lines. The crew was made POW. By the end of the day another Group, III./2. Aé., had left for France.

On the 15th, three Fiat CR 42s of II./2. Aé. protected the photo-reconnaissance by a Fairey Fox of II./1. Aé. (Adjt. Greindl/S/Lt. Verheughe) along the KW-line. Near Mechelen the Fiats were attacked by Bf 109s of 8./JG 3 and the mission had to be cancelled. The Fox (O.38) was also attacked, but the pilot managed to return to base. Meanwhile the three Fiats were outnumbered by the Bf 109s. Lt. Goffin damaged one of the fighters, but had to break off the fight as he was himself pursued by a Bf 109. It was the last fight of the Fiat CR 42 in Belgian airspace. In the evening the Group of Maj. Lamarche was ordered to prepare for movement to France.

During the day the Aéronautique Militaire made a total of 19 reconnaissance flights. Only one could be protected by a platoon of fighters. Most of the crews were tasked to observe the German movements along the Albert Canal and to the east of Antwerp. The observers returned with valuable information. During these flights, the Foxes, Renards and Battle encounter

Hawker Hurricane H-27 was badly shot up during the raid on Schaffen. The plane was lost and left behind.

P. Taghon coll.

Hurricane H-29 at Schaffen airfield. This plane, flown by Sgt. Siroux, was one of the three Hurricanes to escape to Beauvechain.
P. Taghon coll.

very heavy flak. Seven planes were shot down. At 06.00 h three Foxes of I./1. Aé. took off for the Albert Canal, not one returned. Near Holsbeek, a Fox of 7,/III./3. Aé. (Sgt. Soete/Capt de Briey) attacked German infantry with machine-gun fire. The plane made several passes, and was finally hit by groundfire. The crew was killed. Two more planes return with heavy damage to their bases and were written off. The human cost was also high, with four crew members killed, four wounded and two taken POW.

Next day several Squadrons had to change bases and so only six missions were flown along the Albert Canal, the KW-line and the Antwerp-Mechelen-Leuven area. One Fairey Fox of II./1.Aé (Sgt. Van Lierde/Capt. Willemaers) and one Renard R.31 of VI./1. Aé (Sgt. Rigole/S/Lt. Walch) were lost, the crews wounded. In the evening the remaining fighters of the Aéronautique

Pilots of the Hurricane Squadron pose before one of the planes at Steene-Oostende airfield during an exercise. Sitting from left Sgt. Lelarge, 1/Sgt. Doperé, ?, Adjt. Duchateau, Sgt. Libert, Sgt. Lelievre; standing from left, Adjt. Borisewitz, Capt. Van den Hove, Capt. Charlier, 1/Sgt. Siroux, Sgt. Lieutenant.
P. Taghon coll.

30 Fighters ...

Aéronautique Militaire

Destroyed Koolhoven of 4th School Squadron at Goetsenhoven airfield.
P. Taghon coll.

Militaire, six Fiat CR 42s and 8 Fireflies of II./2. Aé, left Aalter for Norrent Fontes. The Aéronautique Militaire was thereby reduced to a total of 45 reconnaissance planes of I./ 1. Aé, II./1. Aé., V./1. Aé., VI./1. Aé. and III./3. Aé.

The weakness of the Aéronautique Militaire obliged the E.MG.A. on the 17th to cut down the reconnaissance flights. The flights could no longer be ordered by the Army Corps and only three were flown. Two Fairey Foxes of II./1. Aé. observed the KW-line and the Leuven-Mechelen-Brussel area. One Battle of III./3. Aé. operated along the Dyle river. All planes returned safely.

During the morning of the 18th, Aalter airfield was raided by a large formation of He 111s of I./KG 4. The SC 50 bombs and machine-gun fire destroyed or damaged all remaining Fairey Foxes of II./1. Aé. and Fairey Battles of III./3.Aé. The airpower of the Aéronautique Militaire was thus reduced to three poorly equipped reconnaissance squadrons.

From their bases at Zwevezele and Ursel these Squadrons flew on that day 8 flights for the E.M.G.A. Three crews were tasked to observe

Renard R. 31 of V./1. Aé. during a training flight above Bierset airfield.
P. Taghon coll.

Fighters ... 31

*Line-up of the Renard R.31s of V./1. Aé. at Rierset.
P. Taghon coll.*

the Antwerp area, where German troop were crossing the Schelde. One of the planes made a crash-landing at Zwevezele airfield. The observer, Sgt. Crabus, was killed.

The 19th was a quite calm day for the Aéronautique Militaire, only 3 flights were made in the Gent-Terneuzen area. All crews returned to their bases. The following day, 7 flights were completed. Again no enemy fighters were met. The remaining Fiat CR 42s of II./2. Aé. arrived at Chartres and the French authorities asked the pilots to contribute to the defence of the airfield. S/Lt. Offenberg, 1/Sgt. Jottard and 1/Sgt. Maes took off for a first patrol in French service. The 21st of May brought no change. Six flights were made without losses. The Fiat CR 42s made 3 "vols d'interdiction" over Chartres, here also there was no sign of the Luftwaffe.

Over the following three days a total of 13 flights were made, 4 on the 22nd, 5 on the 23rd and another 4 on the 24th. Most of the crews returned with valuable information. Two planes were lost. On the 22nd, a Renard R.31 of VI./1. Aé. (Sgt. Bailly/Lt. Warmont) was shot down at Pecq, the crew killed. On the following day, a Fox of I./1. Aé. was posted missing. The crew (Sgt. De Greef/Lt. Keuleers) were tasked to observe German movements near Harelbeke. They did not return to Oostend and up to this day no sign of them was ever found.

During the 25th six missions were completed, three by a Fox and three by a Renard. Four crews observed the German bridgeheads on the Lys, two operated along the canal de dérivation. Although fighter escort promised by the RAF did not show up, Adjt. Vandenweghe/S/Lt. Delbrouck returned with valuable aerial pictures of the area Maldegem-Eeklo-Balgerhoeke. They received the personal congratulations of General Van den Berghe. The most spectacular operation, unique for the Aé. Militaire, was made by Lt. Haubert. Near Courtrai, the fire of the German artillery was led by

32 Fighters ...

a balloon and one single plane had to attack it. Lt. Haubert volunteered for the dangerous mission. He took off in the early morning in a Fairey Fox. A first attempt to destroy the balloon failed, as it was not in the air. During the afternoon Lt. Haubert made a second try, but his plane was shot up by flak and his machine-guns seemed not to be effective at all.

On the 26th the Aéronautique Militaire ordered four reconnaissance flights along the canal de dérivation. All crews returned. After a flight from France, a Fairey Fox was destroyed in a landing accident at Steene airfield. The crew (1/Sgt. Hodeige/S/Lt. Rousseau) was only slightly injured. Next day the Aéronautique Militaire made its last two flights. A Renard R.31 of V./1. Aé. (Sgt. Bruylants/Corp. Charlier) was to observe the Germans in the Maldegem-Eeklo region. They were attacked by a Staffel of Bf 109s, but escaped in the clouds and return safely to Lombardsijde. A Fox of I./ 1.Aé (Adjt. Lems/Lt. Franco) was also send to Eeklo. The plane carried a load of 60 SEGA-grenades, and after the reconnaissance mission, the crew made a successful attack on German infantry.

In the evening General Hiernaux visited Steene airfield. He told Cdt. Burniat that the end was near. The crews hoped to get an order to evacuate to England. They spent the night waiting near their planes. Next morning the Belgian Army capitulated. All remaining planes had to be destroyed. Lt. Haubert disobeyed and tried to take-off. His plane was not warmed up, and he was wounded when it crashed.

The Fiats of II./2. Aé. remained at Chartres airfield and for several day, collaborating with the French for airfield defence. Daily, several interception-flights were made and on the 3rd June, Lt. Goffin and 1/Sgt. Jottard attacked a Do 17. The plane was damaged. On the 10th, Adjt. Moreau managed to place several bursts into a lone reconnaissance plane.

Bf 109 of JG 3, after a crash-landing at Langemark.

P. Taghon coll.

Order of Battle of the Aéronautique Militaire 10.05.1940

Unit	Commander	Peace-time base	Wartime base	Aircraft
1. Aé	Col. Foidart	Bierset	Thisnes	
I./1.Aé	Cdt. Burniat	Deurne	Hingene	10 Fairey Fox Rolls Royce
II./1. Aé	Cdt. Gobert	Goetsenhoven	Glabbee	12 Fairey Fox Rolls Royce, 1 Morane
III./1. Aé	Cdt. Tyou	Goetsenhoven	Jeneffe	10 Fairey Fox Hispano, 1 Morane
IV./1. Aé	Cdt. Lahaye	Goetsenhoven	Goetsenhoven	9 Fairey Fox Hispano, 1 Morane
V./1. Aé	Cdt. Breulhez	Bierset	Duras	11 Renard R. 31, 1 SV 5
VI./1. Aé	Cdt. Dumonceau	Bierset	Hannut	10 Renard R.31, 1 Morane, 3 SV 5
2. Aé.	Col. de Woelmont	Nivelles	Brustem	
I./2.Aé.	Maj. Hendrickx	Schaffen	Beauvechain	15 Gloster Gladiator, 11 Hurricane
II./2.Aé.	Maj. Lamarche	Nivelles	Brustem	23 Fiat CR 42
III./2.Aé.	Maj. De Bock	Nivelles	Vissenaken	28 Fairey Fox Hispano
3. Aé.	Col. Hugon	Evere	Neerhespen	
I./3.Aé.	Maj. Duchâteau	Evere	Neerhespen	18 Fairey Fox Rolls Royce
II./3.Aé.	Maj. Weekers	Evere	Maldegem	6 Fairey Battle*
III./3.Aé	Maj. Piot	Evere	Belsele	8 Fairey Battle (5./III./3. Aé.) 9 Fairey Fox Hispano(7./III./3. Aé.)

* transferred on the 10.05.1940 to the 5./III./3. Aé.

Victories of the Aéronautique Militaire 10.05. - 10.06.1940

Date	Time	Pilot	Unit	Type destroyed	Place	Confirmation
10.05	04.50	Capt. van de Hove	2./I./2. Aé.	He 111 KG 27	Brussel	none
	05.30	Capt. de Callatay	3./II./2. Aé.	Ju 52 17./KGzbV 5	Alken	none
	06.00	Lt. Goffin	3./II./2.Aé.	Bf 109 2/JG 1 Lt. Dutel	Waremme	OJR N° 171 30/07/1940
	06.30	S/Lt. Offenberg	4./II./2. Aé	Do 17 II./KG 77	Waremme	none
	06.30	1/Sgt. Maes	4./II./2. Aé	Do 17 II./KG 77	Waremme	none
	09.00	Lt. Dufossez	5/III./2.Aé.	Bf 109 3/JG 27 Fw. Hoppe	St-Trond	none
	14.40	Lt. de Merode	4./II./2. Aé	Do 17 2(F)/123 Oblt. von Schaessler	Waremme	Déc. Aé. 17 27/01/1947
11.05	06.02	1/Sgt. Winand	1/I./2.Aé	Bf 109	Sichem	none
14.05	13.00	Capt. de Callatay	3./II./2. Aé	Bf 109, 8/JG 3	Fleurus	Déc. Aé. 24 27/01/1947
	13.00	Sgt. Michotte	4./II./2. Aé	Bf 109, 8/JG 3	Fleurus	none
	13.00	Sgt. de Moerlose	4./II./2. Aé	bomber	Fleurus	none
15.05	13.20	Lt. Goffin	3./II./2. Aé	Bf 109	Mechelen	OJR N° 171 30/07/1940
03.06	13.40	Lt. Goffin	3./II./2. Aé	bomber	Chartres	none
	13.40	Lt. Goffin	3./II./2. Aé	bomber	Chartres	none
10.06	-	Adjt. Moreau	4./II./2. Aé	recce-plane	Chartres	none

He 111 of KGr 126 (Oblt. Fr. Sawade), shot down by Morane of GC III/3 on the 12 May at Hoogerheide (Netherlands).

P. Taghon coll.

Map of German advance on 27 May 1940.
Map was originally published in "Wehrmachtberichte Weltgeschichte, Der Krieg 1939/40" by Verlag Die Wehrmacht K. G., Berlin, 1941

RAF Fighters in France 1939-40
by Roger Wallsgrove

Even before the declaration of war on September 3rd 1939, plans had been made to move several squadrons to France. Of the fighter units, 1, 73, 85 and 87 Squadrons were detailed to go to France in August, with their Hurricanes, as the Air Component of the British forces, and flew across to French bases in early September. Initially all were part of 60 Fighter Wing, but 1 and 73 Sqns were soon detached to join the Advanced Air Striking Force (AASF), to support the Blenheims and Battles of that force. Here they came under 67 Fighter Wing. To replace them, two Auxiliary Air Force units, 607 and 615 Sqns flying Gladiators, were despatched to France in November under 61 Fighter Wing. These two units eventually converted to Hurricanes, but only just before the German attack, and could not be considered to be fully proficient on the newer type.

The Hurricanes of these squadrons were not entirely combat ready. Many still had fixed-pitch propellers, and non-ejector exhausts; none had pilot armour or self-sealing fuel tanks. The importance of the latter items rapidly became apparent once the shooting started. The squadrons had all been trained in the sterile and inflexible tactics devised by the "top brass", based on some strange ideas about modern aerial warfare. Combat between

Author's note: RAF operations over France in this period have been described in great detail in a number of books (see bibliography), and this chapter should be considered no more than a brief summary of those authors' researches. For more details, consult the books listed.

Destroyed Hurricanes left behind on an airfield in France
T. Kopański coll.

Spitfire I K9912 YT-O of 65 Squadron, Pilot P/O K. G. Hart, after a forced landing on the Dunkirk beach burnt out his plane.
via W. Matusiak

The visit of King George V to the AASF Squadrons in France 1940.
SHAA via Belcarz

300mph+ monoplane fighters was considered impractical, so all tactics were based on attacks on bombers flying straight and level. (Strange how history repeats itself – the USAF and USN thought supersonic fighters wouldn't/couldn't dogfight, and learned a hard lesson over Vietnam.) That the bombers might defend themselves didn't seem to have occurred to the tacticians, let alone the idea that they might try to manoeuvre to escape attack. The standard "vic" formation of three fighters looked pretty, but had serious disadvantages in combat, soon discovered by the pilots.

In addition the initial gun harmonisation was less than ideal. The so-called "Dowding Spread" was the norm, giving a wide pattern designed to be effective, against large bombers, at 400 yards (369m). Sqn Ldr "Bull" Halahan of 1 Sqn changed the unit's aircraft to a more concentrated pattern, converging at 250 yards (231m). When it became clear that 1 Squadron were more successful at hitting Luftwaffe aircraft, the new harmonisation pattern was adopted widely both in the UK and in France.

By the time of the German attack in May 1940, the squadrons were established at the following bases, having moved around somewhat after their initial move to France. 1 Sqn commanded by Sqn Ldr P.J.H. Halahan, were at Vassincourt, 50 miles from Reims, having moved backwards an forwards between this base and Berry-au-Bac, with 73 Sqn commanded by

Sqn Ldr J.W.C. More at Rouvres, near Verdun. 85 Sqn (Sqn Ldr J.O.W Oliver) and 87 Sqn (Sqn Ldr J.S. Dewar) were at Lille/Seclin, with some of the latter squadron's aircraft detached to Senon to operate with 2 Sqn's Lysanders. 607 (County of Durham) Sqn (Sqn Ldr L.E. Smith) and 615 (County of Surrey) Sqn (Sqn Ldr J.R. Kayll, who replaced Sqn Ldr A. Vere-Harvey in April) were based at Vitry-en-Artois, though in May 1940 615 Sqn were at Abbeville re-equipping with Hurricanes.

During the "Phoney War" period, all these units saw action, mostly intercepting individual reconnaissance aircraft or small numbers of bombers. 1 Sqn's first victory came on 30 October 1939 when "Boy" Mould shot down a Do17, and this was followed by another 25 claims. 73 Sqn made

Above:
Close up shot of a destroyed AASF Hurricane.

Below.
Another destroyed and abandoned Hurricane. A Fairey Battle is visible in the background.
Both photos
T. Kopański coll.

Remains of a Hurricane, somewhere in France.
T. Kopański coll.

Opposite page top:
A classic early wartime propaganda photo, showing pilots and Gladiators in France 1940. Note the roundel types and the camouflage demarcation.
SHAA via Belcarz.

Opposite page middle:
Remains of a Lysander, with a Hurricane in the background.
T. Kopański coll.

30 claims, and in Flg Off E.J. "Cobber" Kain, a New Zealander, had the first RAF ace of the war. Kain became something of a media hero, to the RAF's discomfort. Nov 23rd was a big day for both units, 1 Sqn claiming two Do17s and one He111 and 73 Sqn claiming three Do17s. One RAF pilot was killed. By this time the need for seat armour was clear, and Sqn Ldr Halahan fitted armour from a wrecked Battle to his aircraft. "Expert" opinion back in the UK suggested armour would unbalance the Hurricane by shifting the c-of-g, but Halahan disproved this, and subsequently Hurricanes were equipped with seat armour, saving many lives.

85 Sqn's first victory came on 21 November, and 87 Sqn's on 2nd November. There don't appear to be any claims from the Gladiator squadrons, but there is one story in this regard. A Luftwaffe pilot apparently shot down by a Gladiator and captured, complained that he would never live it down – "shot down by a biplane piloted by a barrister"!

Total claims by the RAF fighters up to May 10th were 60 confirmed, 16 probable and 22 damaged. Luftwaffe records indicate the loss of 35 aircraft (60-100% damage) with 14 suffering less than 60% damage. Whether the German pilots always correctly identified their attackers is a moot point! Very few clashes with Messerschmitt Bf109s were reported.

The Luftwaffe at this stage were not the only "enemy" – whereas 8 aircraft were lost to this source, 9 were shot down by the French (air-to-air or AA fire) and 13 lost to accidents! Aircraft recognition by the RAF, the Armée de l'Air and by ground forces left much to be desired – at least one He112 was claimed by the RAF, and one attack on a single German aircraft by several pilots identified it as a Do17, He111 and Ju88! The AASF Hurricanes were painted with French-style rudder stripes to help overcome air-to-air recognition problems. They also dispensed with unit codes, just using the aircraft letter, whereas Air Component Hurricanes and Gladiators retained theirs.

40 Fighters ...

RAF Fighters

Below:
Hurricane left on an airfield in France.
T. Kopański coll.

Fighters ... *41*

Above: Spitfire I N3295, of 222 Squadron, pilot P/O G G A Davies, after a forced landing on 31 May 1940 at Dunkirk beach.

via W. Matusiak

Below: Early production Hurricane (note two blade propeller), also abandoned on a French airfield.

T. Kopański coll.

Destroyed Gladiator in France, 1940. A He 111 and a German look on.
T. Kopański coll.

Following the German attack on May 10th, several other RAF units were thrown into the battle, in addition to operations from UK bases. 3 and 79 Sqns arrived in France, to be based at Merville, and 501 Sqn joined the AASF at Betheniville on that day. 504 Sqn later joined the Air Component, and reinforcements from 11 Group in the UK operated from French bases during the campaign, including elements from the following squadrons: 17, 32, 56, 111, 145, 151, 213, 229, 242, 245, 253, and 601, all flying Hurricanes.

10th May – the German attack begins. Most airfields were bombed, and 615 Sqn lost two aircraft on the ground. 73 Sqn moved to Reims-Champagne, and 1 Sqn to Berry-au-Bac. AASF – 47 sorties, 5 losses; Air Component –161 sorties, 2 losses, 8 damaged.

Remains of a Hurricane and a Gladiator (to the right) in France.
T. Kopański coll.

Fighters ... **43**

The sparse remains of a Gladiator Mk I in France, destroyed on the ground, is inspected by a German soldier after the British had left.
T. Kopański coll.

Total claims: 60 confirmed/ 16 probable/ 22 damaged. Luftwaffe records: 35 (60-100%)/ 14 (<60% damage).

11th May – 17 Sqn from 11 Group involved in the fighting, with 6 claims and 5 losses. Overall 13 Hurricanes lost.
Total claims: 55/5/6; Luftwaffe records: 28/6

12th May – the first time Bf109s were met in any numbers, shooting down half of the 13 Hurricanes lost. In return 10 Bf109s were claimed, against one actually lost and one damaged.
Total claims: 52/7/1; Luftwaffe records: 23/4

13th May – 10 Hurricanes lost, 6 to Bf109s.
Total claims: 26/11/0; Luftwaffe records: 16/5

14th May – replacement Hurricanes arriving at this time included some with no gunsights, and with guns not harmonised; but they now had Rotol constant speed propellers. 27 Hurricanes were lost, 22 to Bf109s, with 15 pilots killed. "Cobber" Kain shot down a Potez 631 in error, mistaking it for a Bf110. Ju87B Stukas were encountered in large numbers for the first time, and 15 were claimed shot down.
Total claims: 60/14/9; Luftwaffe records: 38/8

15th May – 1 Sqn attacked a massed formation of Do17s and Bf110s, claiming at least 6 of the latter. 21 Hurricanes were lost during the day, with 5 pilots killed.
Total claims: 35/7/8; Luftwaffe records: 22/5

44 Fighters ...

16th May – the equivalent of 4 squadrons were dispatched to France, over Dowding's strenuous objections. One Flight each from 56, 229, 242, 253, 601 and 245 Squadrons came over. Some of the 253 Sqn Hurricanes were early fabric-winged machines, with 2-blade props, ineffective radios, and no armour. I Sqn moved to Vraux, to join 114 Sqn Blenheims. 13 Hurricanes went down, with 5 pilots killed.
Total claims: 14/1/9; Luftwaffe records: 7/2

17th May – aircraft from 11 Group were active, with elements from 151, 37, 601, 111 and 213 Sqns. Ju87s were again on the menu, with 151 Sqn claiming 7 and 17 Sqn 3. 16 Hurricanes were lost, 3 in accidents, but no pilots were killed.
Total claims: 39/13/3; Luftwaffe records: 26/2

18th May – a bad day for the Hurricanes. 33 shot down, for the loss of 7 pilots, with 5 made PoW and 4 wounded. 29 Bf110s were claimed, but in reality only 12 were shot down by the RAF.
Total claims: 57/20/20; Luftwaffe records: 39/7

19th May – another bad day, with 22 Hurricanes lost and 13 force-landed. 8 pilots killed, 7 wounded, 3 PoW. Again Bf109s were the main cause, with 24 to their credit. 14 Bf109s were claimed, and 14 He111s of KG54 were shot down by the RAF, so it was not all one way. The original personnel of 1 and 73 Sqns were sent back to the UK, having seen more than their share of action.
Total claims: 74/25/13; Luftwaffe records: 47/9

20th May - 12 Hurricanes lost, 7 to AA fire. 3 pilots killed, 1 PoW.
Total claims: 23/5/12; Luftwaffe records: 15/3

Remains of a Hurrciane.
T. Kopański coll.

Fighters ... 45

Another propaganda photo for the folks back home – taken on the same occasion as the photo on page 41. One hopes that the Gladiators weren't lined up so neatly and unprotected normally!
IWM

21st May – 11 Group were again involved, with elements from 17, 151, 253 and 229 Sqns. Spitfires were active over the French coast, from 54 and 74 Sqns. 3 Hurricanes were lost, with 1 pilot dead and 1 PoW.
Total claims: 4/0/0; Luftwaffe records: 3/0

(From this time on, much of the action over France involved UK-based Hurricanes and Spitfires. As the Luftwaffe records do not allow a distinction between these and French-based aircraft, and many of the RAF units lost their records in the retreat, precise details of the AASF/Air Component operations and victories are obscure.)

22nd May – Hurricane pilots claimed 7 Hs126s, though none actually were lost, and 6 (+ 2 probable) Bf109s, and 10 (+5) Ju87Bs, 6 of which were actually lost. Five Hurricanes were lost.

23rd May – ten Hurricanes lost, versus 6 Bf109s claimed.

24th May – two Hurricanes lost, with 2 claims.

25th May – six Hurricanes lost, with 2 pilots killed and 1 PoW

Sporadic fighting continued, with the major battles over Dunkirk as the BEF escaped from France (26th May - 1st June). Elements of the RAF (1, 73 and 501 Sqns) remained in France until mid-June, constantly moving west to escape from the advancing German forces. 17 and 242 Sqns joined them in June, just in time to be part of the final move back to the UK via the Channel Islands. "Cobber" Kain, one of the leading aces of the campaign, was killed in a flying accident on the day he was due to return to the UK. Making one last Hurricane flight, he misjudged his aerobatic display and spun in.

Only 66 Hurricanes returned to the UK, of 452 sent out, and almost all of the ground equipment was lost. 56 pilots were killed, 36 wounded and 18 ended up as PoW. During May the Hurricane squadrons claimed some 500 victories and over 120 probables, against 215 Hurricanes shot down. Actual Luftwaffe losses to the French-based RAF units in May appear to have been 299 plus 65+ seriously damaged.

The Hurricane operations were mostly in small numbers, 3 or 6 aircraft, against larger formations, and were poorly coordinated. Despite the bravery and exceptional efforts of the ground and air crews, little was achieved, but numerous valuable lessons were learned, not all of them immediately acted on by the RAF generally. The deployment of Hurricanes from many different squadrons probably helped in training more pilots in modern air warfare, but the loss of so many aircraft was a serious matter, considering the big fight about to start over southern England.

For all the problems and failures, one must not forget the heroic efforts of the ground crews in France. Operating under far from ideal conditions, on makeshift airfields (many were literally fields!), and having to move rapidly to escape the advancing German army, they nonetheless kept a large number of Hurricanes in the air. The eventual failure of the enterprise was not their fault. With the loss of almost all the squadron records, we cannot know the full details, but minor miracles were undoubtedly achieved.

Arguments continue as to whether a bigger RAF presence in France would have made a difference, but most commentators agree that this would have merely lead to greater losses of men and machines, and seriously weakened the RAF. Given the makeshift airfields used much of the time in France, it is clear that sending Spitfires would have been a huge mistake, and the Hurricanes did a fine job despite the problems. The Battle of France was lost, but the Battle of Britain was another story…

This Hurricane had been abandoned in almost in perfect condition, but was later stripped down by souvenir hunters.
T. Kopański coll.

Hurricane left on a French airfield. Note the two blade propeller.
    T. Kopański coll.

Bibliography
Twelve Days in May, Brian Cull and Bruce Lander with Heinrich Weiss. Grub Street, London, 1995.
Fighter Pilot, Paul Richey. Pan Books, London, 1969.
A.A.S.F., Charles Gardner. Hutchinson & Co., London, 1940.
The Air Battle of Dunkirk, Norman Franks. William Kimber, 1983.
Fledgling Eagles, Christopher Shores et al. Grub Street, London.
Acknowledgements
Many thanks to George Paul for the loan of "A.A.S.F." by C.Gardner.

Spitfire I, probably of 54 Squadron, on the beach close to Nieuport.
    via W. Matusiak

48 Fighters ...

L' Armée de l'Air in the 1940 campaign
by Bartłomiej Belcarz

The "Phoney War" period made it clear to the French High Command that the equipment of fighter units needed rapid modernisation. At the time when France entered the war, on 3 September 1939, the French Air Force (Armée de l'Air; AdA) had in its inventory the relatively modern Morane MS.406 and Curtiss Hawk H 75A, which equipped 15 squadrons (Groupe de Chasse; GC) of the AdA. A further 8 squadrons used the obsolete Dewoitine D.501/510s, Spad 510s, and Nieuport Delage NiD 622/629s. Moreover, 4 squadrons were equipped with Potez 631 fighters. There was a total of 472 modern aircraft of varying combat value on metropolitan French airfields. The best among these, the Hawks (a total of 97) equipped only 4 squadrons (GCs I/4, II/4, I/5, II/5).

Allied commanders failed to draw correct conclusions from the fall of Poland in 1939. The period of relative peace that lasted from October 1939 until May 1940 put the vigilance of the French to sleep. Although they modernised their fighter aviation a little, by introducing the Bloch 151/152 into front-line units, there was hardly any increase in the numbers available to the AdA HQ.

Morane Saulniers on the assembly line in Nantes. Photo was taken during the visit of Minister Guy Le Chambre in May 1939.
B. Belcarz coll.

The fighter force was divided into operational zones (Zone des Operations Aeriennes; ZOA) in which individual fighter groups (Groupment de Chasse; Grpmt) operated. The table below lists all the units and their equipment as of 10 May 1940.

Unit	Aircraft type	Total/serviceable	Base	Operational Zone/Fighter Group
GC I/1	MB 152	23/15	Chantilly les Aigles	ZOAN/Grpmt 21
GC II/1	MB 152	25/18	Buc	ZOAN/Grpmt 21
GC III/1	MS 406	30/20	Norrent - Fontes	ZOAN/Grpmt 25
GC I/2	MS 406	31/27	Toul - Ochey	ZOAE/Grpmt 22
GC II/2	MS 406	26/22	Laon	ZOAN/Grpmt 23
GC III/2	MS 406	34/28	Cambrai Nigernies	ZOAN/Grpmt 23
GC III/3	MS 406	28/23	Beauvais - Tillé	ZOAN/Grpmt 21
GC I/4	H 75	30/29	Wez - Thuisy	ZOAN/Grpmt 23
GC II/4	H 75	31/29	Xaffévilliers	ZOAE/Grpmt 22
GC I/5	H 75	29/25	Suippes	ZOAN/Grpmt 23
GC II/5	H 75	26/14	Toul - Croix de Metz	ZOAE/Grpmt 22
GC I/6	MS 406	25/12	Marseille - Marignane	ZOAA
GC II/6	MS 406	34/20	Anglures - Vouarces	ZOAE/Grpmt 22
GC III/6	MS 406	36/30	Chissey s/Loue	ZOAS/Grpmt24
GC II/7	MS 406	35/24	Luxeuil - St Sauveur	ZOAS/Grpmt24
GC III/7	MS 406	34/23	Vitry le François	ZOAE/Grpmt 22
GC I/8	MB 152	37/20	Verlaine en Haye	ZOAE/Grpmt 22
GC II/8	MB 152	19/11	Calais - Marck	ZOAN/Grpmt 25
GC III/9	MB 151/152	11/9	Lyon - Bron	ZOAA
GC I/10	MB 151/152	31/20	Rouen Boos	ZOAN/Grpmt 21
GC III/10	MB 151/152	39/18	Le Havre Octeville	ZOAN/Grpmt 21
ECMJ 1/16	Potez 631	17/10	Wez - Thuisy	ZOAN/Grpmt 23
ECN 1/13	Potez 631	12/8	Meaux - Esbly	ZOAN/Night fighter Grpmt
ENC 2/13	Potez 631	11/7	Melun - Villaroche	ZOAN/Night fighter Grpmt
ECN 3/13	Potez 631	12/10	Le Plessis Belleville	ZOAN/Night fighter Grpmt
ECN 4/13	Potez 631	12/7	Betz - Bouillancy	ZOAN/Night fighter Grpmt
ENC 5/13	Potez 631	11/11	Loyettes	ZOAA
TOTAL		**689/490**		

Source: Batailles Aeriennes No 7, La campagne de France (La bataille du Nord)

Unidentified Bloch MB 152 captured by the Germans.
                    T. Kopański coll.

The aerial operations can be divided into several phases.

PHASE 1 – 10-26 May 1940
Battle of Northern France.

This phase commenced with the German attack against Holland (18th Army), Belgium (6, 4, 12 Armies), and Luxembourg (16 Army). This move allowed the Germans to avoid the French fortifications along the French-German frontier, known as the Maginot Line. This strike was aimed at the weak point of the Allied defences. After the initial surprise during the first hours of the war, the Allies prepared counter-measures by throwing their bomber units into action, and by moving their fighter units into Belgium.

On 10 May the AdA lost 9 MS 406s, 5 H 75As and 1 MB 152. The same day 36 German aircraft were shotdown. The initial days saw very fierce fighting in the air. The Battle of Flanders started in earnest.

The scale of the conflict is best shown in the listing of the French fighter aviation claims and losses.

Curtis Hawk 75A stripped by souvenir hunters.
T. Kopański coll.

Below:
Morane MS 406 of
GC III/2 at Cambrai.
T. Kopański coll.

Day	Number of claims	Types of claimed aircraft	Number of losses	Types of lost aircraft
10/5/40	36	Bf 109 - 2 Bf 110 - 2 Do 17 - 13 He 111 - 18 Ju 88 - 1	15	MS 406 - 9 H 75A - 5 MB 152 - 1
11/5/40	24	Bf 109 - 6 Bf 110 - 1 Do 17 - 3 Do 215 - 1 He 111 - 13	18	MS 406 - 10 H 75A - 5 MB 152 - 3
12/5/40	34	Bf 110 - 5 Do 17 - 6 He 111 - 9 Ju 88 - 2 Ju 87 - 11 Hs 123 - 1	13	MB 152 - 3 MS 406 - 8 H 75A - 2
13/5/40	25	Bf 109 - 7 Bf 110 - 3 Do 17 - 1 He 111 - 8 Hs 126 - 6	13	MS 406 - 12 H 75A - 1
14/5/40	46	Bf 109 - 10 Bf 110 - 16 Do 17 - 4 He 111 - 9 Ju 87 - 2 Hs 126 - 5	28	MB 152 - 16 MS 406 - 7 D 520 - 2 H 75A - 3
15/5/40	25	Bf 109 - 7 Bf 110 - 6 Do 17 - 7 Do 215 - 1 He 111 - 1 Hs 126 - 2 Other - 1	23	MB 152 - 4 MS 406 - 9 D 520 - 8 H 75A - 2
16/6/40	18	Bf 110 - 5 Do 17 - 4 Do 215 - 1 He 111 - 1 Hs 126 - 5 Other -2	11	MB 152 - 4 MS 406 - 6 H 75A - 1
17/5/40	17	Bf 109 - 9 Bf 110 - 2 Do 17 - 1 He 111 - 2 Hs 126 - 3	19	MB 152 - 10 MS 406 - 3 H 75A - 3 Potez 631 - 3
18/5/40	24	Bf 109 - 5 Do 17 - 3 He 111 - 12 Hs 126 - 4	11	MS 406 - 5 D 520 - 1 H 75A - 3 MB 152 - 2
19/5/40	17	Bf 109 - 2 Bf 110 - 1 Do 17 - 2 Do 215 - 1 He 111 - 6 Hs 126 - 5	5	MS 406 - 4 MB 152 - 1

Source: J. and P. Martin, Ils étaient la…

Day	Number of claims	Types of claimed aircraft	Number of losses	Types of lost aircraft
20/5/40	17	Bf 109 - 4 Bf 110 - 2 Do 17 - 2 Do 215 - 3 He 111 - 3 Ju 88 - 1 Ju 87 - 1 Other - 1	10	MB 152 - 3 MS 406 - 6 H 75A - 1
21/5/40	16	Bf 109 - 5 Bf 110 - 2 Do 17 - 5 Do 215 - 1 He 111 - 2 Hs 126 - 1	25	MB 152 - 6 MS 406 - 12 D 520 - 6 H 75A - 1
22/5/40	11	Do 17 - 1 Ju 87 - 8 Hs 126 - 2	2	D 520 - 2
23/5/40	1	Hs 126 - 1	3	D 520 - 2 MS 406 - 1
24/5/40	8	Bf 109 - 4 Do 17 - 1 Do 215 - 1 He 111 - 1 Hs 126 - 1	9	MS 406 - 8 Potez 631 - 1
25/5/40	11	Bf 109 - 1 Do 17 - 5 He 111 - 2 Ju 87 - 2 Hs 126 - 1	10	MS 406 - 6 D 520 - 1 H 75A - 3
26/5/40	22	Bf 109 - 11 Do 17 - 3 He 111 - 5 Hs 126 - 3	8	MB 152 - 2 MS 406 - 3 H 75A - 3
TOTAL	352	Bf 109 - 73 Bf 110 - 45 Do 17 - 61 Do 215 - 9 He 111 - 92 Ju 88 - 4 Ju 87 - 24 Hs 126 - 39 Hs 123 - 1 Other - 4	223	MS 406 - 109 H 75A - 33 MB 152 - 55 D 520 - 22 Potez 631 - 4

Source: J. and P. Martin, Ils étaient la…

Those first days of the campaign made it clear to the Allies that they were not prepared for the fight. They had wasted the several months since the fall of Poland. Perhaps they thought that Hitler was bluffing once again, but they were wrong. The German war machine was gaining momentum. Although the main attack was aimed at the Low Countries, this did not mean that other areas were safe from air operations. In fact French units were losing much more equipment on the ground than in the air. German

Above:
MS 406s of CIC at Montpellier.
SHAA

Right:
Morane Saulnier MS 406 was the main French fighter in the first months of the war.
T. Kopański coll.

Right:
Ju 88 of unknown unit (probably Ernaufklärung) shot down by Sgt. Doublet of GC III/1.
P. Taghon coll.

L'Armée de L'Air Fighters

Above:
Morane MS 406 no 996 of GC III/3 after a force landing on 16 May 1940 in Vertain. It was the personal aircraft of cne. Trouillard, but on that day was piloted by Adj. Chef Morias.
B. Belcarz coll.

Left:
MS 406 no 923 of GC III/2. Photo was taken at Cambrai airfield.
P. Taghon coll.

Left:
MS 406 no 1019 – personal aircraft of gen. Pinsard. See also colour profile on page 138.
SHAA

Fighters ... 55

MS 406 somewhere in France, 1940
T. Kopański coll.

raids against aerodromes proved particularly effective. On 10 May 1940 alone GC III/2 lost14 Morane 406s in raids and air combats. The German raid of 27 May 1940 against Lagny, the base of GCIII/6, proved extremely successful. It resulted in 16 MS 406s being written off. This was over 50 percent of the total inventory of the unit. This indicates how careless the French were about camouflaging and dispersing their aircraft on the ground.

Another reason behind the German superiority was their aircraft guidance system. For the attacking side this component was not as vital as for the defenders. The first days of the war proved that the French way of homing onto German aircraft was a failure. Frequently French aircraft would only

Curtis Hawk 75A at the German exhibition of captured French armament.
T. Kopański coll.

56 *Fighters ...*

be scrambled after enemy aircraft were spotted by the AA gun crews, but then it was too late for any effective action.

During the initial period of the campaign, the prevailing French tactic was to perform air patrols in order to intercept German aircraft. However, needless to say, this tactic was rather troublesome, as it forced the French to constantly engage most of their air force, with little effectiveness. The loss of air superiority resulted in a change of tactics. The so-called territorial air defence (Défense Aérienne du Territoire, DAT) fighter sections were set up from personnel under training, in order to provide air defence of allocated areas or objects.

PHASE 2 – 27 May-4 June 1940

This phase resembled the operations of the Polish campaign in September 1939. Rapid changes in the military situation forced air force units to constantly re-locate. This was a result of the lightning war on the ground.

After Phase 1 of the German operations ended, when Wehrmacht troops reached the Channel and encircled Allied units at Dunkirk, the German air activity decreased for a short while.

During that time the French attempted to replenish and reinforce their units, and also to change their air defence plans a little. The changed situation put Paris in greatest danger. This led to a concentration of units around the capital city. These units received reinforcements, but largely insufficient.

In order to protect the strategically important military objects (bases, armament factories, aircraft assembly plants) the system of defence units, known as DAT (Défense Aérienne du Territoire), was established. A total of at least 21 such sections were formed. They included French, Polish, Czechoslovak, and Belgian pilots. However, their role should not be overestimated. In most cases the DAT sections were in a much more difficult position than front line units, starting with aircraft allocation problems, up to operational matters. DAT sections were in virtually no position to develop an airspace monitoring network, and very often their aircraft would take off only when a German raid was in progress, and the effectiveness of the defence was minimal. Successes were only achieved when the enemy was encountered, usually by chance, during a patrol.

Most of these sections were made up of French (11 units) and Polish (12 units) pilots. Other DAT sections included Czechs (2 units), and Belgians (2 units).

In most cases the DAT activity proved of little effect. According to French publications (M. Comas) the French pilots of DAT sections could be credited with at least 9 enemy aircraft shot down. Activity of DAT sections of other nationalities is discussed in the chapters on these respective nationalities.

German air attack on the GC I/2 airfield at Damblin on 27 May 1940.
SHAA

Cne. Patric O'Byrne, commander of 1 Esc. GC I/4 and Hawk 75 A-2, serial no. 105. O'Byrne was killed in action on 10 May 1940.
SHAA

Fighters ... 57

Day	Number of claims	Types of claimed aircraft	Number of losses	Types of lost aircraft
27/05/40	1	Do 17 - 1	3	MB 152 - 3
28/05/40	1	Do 17 - 1	-	-
29/05/40	1	Do 17 -1	-	-
30/05/40	-	-	-	-
31/05/40	-	-	5	D 520 - 5
1/06/40	9	He 111 - 5 Do 17 - 1 Hs 126 - 1 Ju 88 - 2	2	H 75A - 1 MS 406 -1
2/06/40	2	He 111 - 1 Do 17 - 1	3	MS 406 -1 MB 151 -1 Potez 631 - 1
3/06/40	17	Bf 109 - 9 Do 215 - 1 Ju 88 - 1 Hs 126 - 1 Bf 110 - 2 Do 17 - 3	18	MB 152 - 10 D 520 - 3 H 75A - 2 MS 406 - 2 Potez 631 - 1
4/06/40	1	Bf 110 - 1	-	-
TOTAL	32	Bf 109 - 9 Bf 110 - 3 Do 17 - 8 He 111 - 6 Hs 126 - 2 Ju 88 - 3 Do 215 - 1	31	MB 151/152 - 14 D 520 - 8 H 75A - 3 MS 406 - 4 Potez 631 - 2

Source: J. and P. Martin, Ils étaient la…..

During late May and early June, air operations over France were of low intensity. This was probably due to German operations mainly focused at that time against Allied forces attempting to evacuate from Dunkirk to Britain. At the same time the French Air Force, after the initial shock of the first German strikes, tried to re-deploy its forces and restore numbers. The time it had was definitely too short for any effective action, though.

This phase was the prelude for the fierce fighting to be fought, mainly in defence of Paris and its surrounding area. The Germans called this operation "Paula".

PHASE 3 – 5-24 June 1940

The French Air Force order of battle on 5 June 1940 is listed in the table below. Compared to 10 May 1940, 5 units had their MS 406s replaced by the modern Dewoitine D 520s. Also, GC III/2 had converted to Curtiss H 75As. This latter change was necessitated by the fact that GC III/2 had lost most of its aircraft during the early phase of the campaign. Moreover, the Caudron C 714-equipped GC 1/145 arrived at the front line. Combat value of these aircraft was doubtful. They presented a lot of engineering problems, which had led the French Minister of Aviation, Guy de Chambre, to ground them on 25 May 1940. However, the unit entered combat, as there was no time to quickly convert it to another aircraft type. For more about the GC 1/145 operations, see chapter "Polish Air Force Fighters in France", page no 97.

The changes in quality did not significantly improve the potential of the French forces. The Dewoitine D 520s were introduced with great haste. Pilots had no time for the necessary training to properly acquaint themselves with the new type. Nevertheless, they were enthusiastic about the D 520. However, on 5 June 1940 the French had only 65 serviceable aircraft of this type.

Curtis Hawk 75A captured by German troops.
T. Kopański coll.

Unidentified Hawk 75A on a makeshift airfield.
SHAA

Unit	Aircraft type	Total/serviceable	Base	Operational Zone/Fighter Group
GC I/1	MB152	20/17	Chantilly	ZOAN/ Grpmt 21
GC II/1	MB152	21/17	Brétigny	ZOAN/ Grpmt 21
GC II/10	MB 151/MB152	21/15	Bernay	ZOAN/ Grpmt 21
GC III/10	MB152	20/15	Deauville	ZOAN/ Grpmt 21
GC I/145	C 714	32/21	Dreux	ZOAN/ Grpmt 21
GC II/8	MB152	8/8	Deauville	ZOAN/ Grpmt 21
GC I/3	D 520	19/13	Meaux-Esbly	ZOAN/ Grpmt 23
GC II/3	D 520	15/10	La Ferté-Gaucher	ZOAN/ Grpmt 23
GC III/3	D 520/MS 406	18(15)/5	Cormeilles en Vexin	ZOAN/ Grpmt 23
GC I/4	H 75	22/20	Evereux-Fauville	ZOAN/ Grpmt 23
GC II/4	H 75	37/30	Orconte	ZOAN/ Grpmt 23
GC I/8	MB 152	22/14	Claye-Soumilly	ZOAN/ Grpmt 23
GC II/9	MB 152	14/9	Connantre	ZOAN/ Grpmt 23
GC III/7	MS 406	28/19	Coulommiers	ZOAN/ Grpmt 23
GC I/6	MS 406	22/16	Lognes	ZOAN/ Grpmt 23
ECN 1/13	Potez 631	**Total**	Moissy-Cramayel	ZOAN/ Grpmt 23
ECN 2/13	Potez 631	**38/15**	Melun-Villaroche	ZOAN/ Grpmt 23
ECN 3/13	Potez 631		Chailly en Biere	ZOAN/ Grpmt 23
ECN 4/13	Potez 631		Melun-Villaroche	ZOAN/ Grpmt 23
ECMJ 1/16	Potez 631		Moissy-Cramael	ZOAN/ Grpmt 23
GC II/6	MB 152	34/27	Chateauroux	ZOAE/ Grpmt 22
GC I/2	MS 406	21/16	Damblain	ZOAE/ Grpmt 22
GC I/5	H 75	26/22	St Dizier	ZOAE/ Grpmt 22
GC II/5	H 75	22/17	Toul Croix-de-Metz	ZOAE/ Grpmt 22
GC III/2	H 75	30/28	Avord	ZOAE/ Grpmt 22
GC II/2	MS 406	30/20	Chissey	ZOAE/ Grpmt 24
GC II/7	D 520	29/27	Avelanges	ZOAE/ Grpmt 24
GC III/1	MS 406	20/?	Valence	ZOAA
GC III/6	MS 406	20/?	Le Luc	ZOAA
GC III/9	MB 151/152	21/18	Lyon-Stolas	ZOAA
ECN 5/13	Potez 631	7/?	Loyettes	ZOAA

Destroyed MS 406, no. 490. Pilot Adj. Guingo of GC III/1 crashed on 3 June 1940.

Belcarz coll.

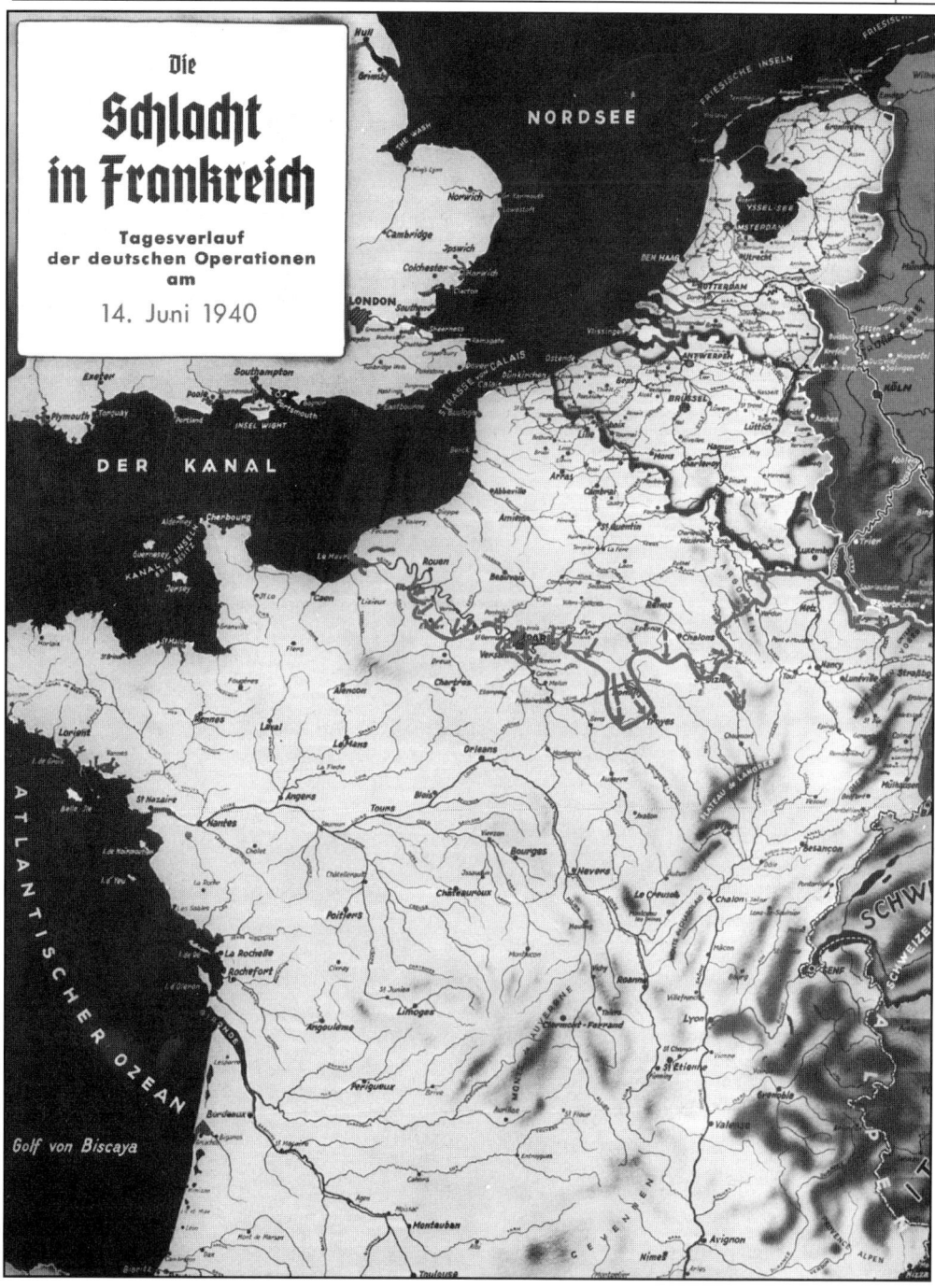

Map of German advance on 14 June 1940.
Map was originally published in "Wehrmachtberichte Weltgeschichte, Der Krieg 1939/40" by Verlag Die Wehrmacht K. G., Berlin, 1941

Operational effort of the French fighter aviation is listed in the table below:

Day	Number of claims	Types of claimed aircraft	Number of losses	Types of lost aircraft
5/06/40	55	Bf 109 - 24 Bf 110 - 3 Do 17 - 1 He 111 - 13 Ju 88 - 3 Hs 126 - 8 Hs 123 - 3	18	MB 151/152 - 4 MS 406 - 4 D 520 - 8 H 75A - 2
6/06/40	28	Bf 109 - 18 Bf 110 - 2 Do 17 - 5 Do 215 -1 Hs 126 - 2	15	MB 152 - 6 D 520 - 1 H 75A - 7 MS 406 - 1
7/06/40	20	Bf 109 - 13 Do 17 - 2 He 111 - 3 Hs 126 - 2	10	D 520 - 1 H 75A - 1 MS 406 - 2 MB 152 -6
8/06/40	24	Bf 109 - 7 He 111 - 1 Ju 87 - 13 Hs 126 - 3	16	MB 152 - 3 MS 406 - 7 H 75A - 4 D 520 - 2
9/06/40	24	Bf 109 - 14 Do 17 - 3 He 111 - 3 Ju 87 - 2 Hs 126 - 2	18	MB 152 - 4 H 75A - 6 D 520 - 1 C 714 - 7
10/06/40	12	Bf 110 - 3 Do 17 - 4 He 111 - 1 Ju 88 - 1 Hs 126 - 3	3	MS 406 - 2 C 714 - 1
11/06/40	6	Do 17 - 2 Hs 126 - 4	8	MB 152 - 4 MS 406 - 3 D 520 - 1
12/06/40	2	Hs 126 -2	-	-
13/06/40	10	Bf 109 - 4 He 111 - 1 Ju 87 - 3 Other - 2	6	H 75A - 3 D 520 -2 MB 152 - 1
14/06/40	5	Do 17 - 1 Do 215 - 1 Hs 126 -3	2	MB 151 -1 Potez 631 - 1
15/06/40	14	Do 17 - 2 He 111 - 1 Ju 88 - 1 Hs 126 - 4 Hs 123 - 1 Other - 5	5	H 75A - 2 D 520 - 3
16/06/40	5	He 111 - 1 Ju 88 - 1 Hs 126 - 3	4	MS 406 - 1 D 520 - 2 H 75A - 1
17/06/40	1	He 111 -1	1	MS 406 - 1
18 - 24/06/40	4	Do 17 - 1 He 111 - 1 Hs 126 - 2	4	MB 152 - 2 MS 406 - 2
TOTAL	210	Bf 109 - 80 Bf 110 - 8 Do 17 - 21 He 111 - 26 Ju 88 - 6 Hs 126 - 38 Hs 123 - 4 Do 215 - 2 Ju 87 - 18 Other - 7	110	MB 151/152 - 31 MS 406 - 23 D 520 - 21 H 75A - 26 C 714 - 8 Potez 631 - 1

62 Fighters ...

Loire 46 at Cazaux airfield.
**P. Rivierre coll.
via K. Chołoniewski**

Operations during the last period of the campaign were marked by the chaos that enveloped the French troops. The fall of Paris was the decisive moment for the breakdown of French morale. When Petain took power, this was the start of surrender negotiations. This allowed France to avoid complete occupation by the Germans, but at the same time it caused a great gap in the Allied block.

During the campaign no less 31 French pilots scored at least 6 victories. Nine of them claimed at least 10 enemy aircraft. All except Sgt Le Nigen and S/Lt Le Gloan flew the American Curtisses.

The top position on the scoreboard is occupied by Edmond Marin La Meslée with 16 victories.

Curtis Hawk 75A captured by the Germans in 1940.
B. Belcarz coll.

Fighters ... 63

Above:
MS 406 no. 593 being assembled at the factory.
PI&SM London

Right:
French pilots pose near a He 111 of KG 55. In the centre is Lt. Augustin Flandi of GC I/8.
P. Taghon coll.

MS 406 no. 973 of **Ecole de Pilotage de Chasse** in Avord. Photo was taken in December 1939.
SHAA

Above:
Morane Saulnier MS 406 at Istres airfield.

SHAA

Below:
Morane Saulnier MS 406 no. 393 (N811) of 3 Esc. GC III/2 at Cambrai airfield. May 1940.

SHAA

Cdt. Geille commander of GC III/2.
B. Belcarz coll.

Edmond Marin La Meslée
The scoreboard of Edmond Marin La Meslée:
1. 11/01/40 – Do-17 shot down, shared with another pilot at Longwy
2. 12/05/40 – Ju 87, individually over Bouillon
3. 12/05/40 – Ju 87, individually over Pouru St-Rémy
4. 12/05/40 – Ju 87, individually over Ste-Cécile
5. 13/05/40 – Bf 109, individually over Stonne
6. 15/05/40 – Hs 126, shared with 6 pilots over Vendresse
7. 16/05/40 – Do 215, shared with 8 pilots over Rethel
8. 18/05/40 – He 111, shared with 2 pilots over Rethel
9. 18/05/40 – He 111, shared with 4 pilots over Ponsart
10. 18/05/40 – He 111, shared with 4 pilots over Laon
11. 19/05/40 – He 111, shared with another pilot over Hesse
12. 24/05/40 – Hs 126, individually over St Loup-Terrier
13. 25/05/40 – Hs 126, shared with 3 pilots over Boult-aux-Bois
14. 26/05/40 – He 111, shared with 8 pilots over Tannay
15. 03/06/40 – Hs 126, shared with 3 pilots over Sommauthe
16. 10/06/40 – Ju 88, shared with 4 pilots over Chatillon sur-Bar

Thus, Marin La Meslée scored 5 individual victories. However, the French method of scoring increased that with the 11 shared kills.

La Meslée was born at Valenciennes on 5 February 1912. After graduating from secondary school he underwent training at the Morane flying school, obtaining his pilot's licence on 1 August 1931. Before being drafted, in November of that year he volunteered for reserve officer's training, and completed this on 20 October 1932. He was initially posted to the 2e Regiment de Chasse at Strasbourg. By the end of the year he signed up for 2 more years. In 1936 he decided to become a career soldier, and was posted, with the rank of Sous Lieutenant, to SPA 67, part of GC I/5.

At the outbreak of war he flew Hawk fighters.

Destroyed Curtis Hawk 75A.
B. Belcarz coll.

In June 1939 GC I/5 was moved to Suippes. For the next 6 months La Meslée had no opportunity to test his ability in combat. His first encounter came on 11 January 1940, when he intercepted a Do 17P of 3.(F)/11over Verdun. This was the first victory of the future ace, albeit shared with Sous Lt Rey.

His next victory, and a triple one, was scored on 12 May, when he downed 3 Ju 87s over the Ardennes. Four more were credited as probables. The following day he shot down a Bf 109E.

Between 15 and 26 May he flew and fought every day. His full scoreboard is listed in the table. His final victory was scored on 10 June, a Ju 88 which crashed at Chatillon du Bar.

On 25 June GC I/5 found itself in Algeria, and ceased flying for 2 and half years. After Operation "Torch", GC I/5 was equipped with P-39 Airacobras and commenced operational flying. These consisted of convoyescort and coastal patrols. During the winter of 1944/1945 La Meslée's unit participated in the liberation of France. La Meslée took command of the unit, which meanwhile changed its name to "Champagne" and re-equipped with P-47 Thunderbolts.

He was shot down and killed by ground fire on 4 February 1945, while leading an attack against a column of vehicles at Hart.

It is difficult to find an unambiguous opinion of the campaign. Probably each participating side had their own views. What is beyond doubt is that in 1940 a myth was shattered, the myth of an invincible France.

MS 406 no. 103 of 4 Esc., GC III/2 being recovered by the Germans.
P. Taghon coll.

MS 406 of GC III/6 at Wez-Thuisy airfield.
SHAA

Above: MS 406 no. 439 "Flandre" with GC I/2 insignia which was used in 1939. In front of the aircraft is Lt. Leenhardt, a pilot of GC III/1.

SHAA

L'Armée de L'Air Fighters

Above:
Take off of MS 406s of 3 Esc. GC II/7, April 1940 at Luxeuil airfield.
SHAA

Left:
D 520 of GC II/7. In the photo is the personal aircraft of Sgt. Jean Doudie's.
Joanne coll.

Right, below:
Curtis Hawk 75 A1 no. 183, personal aircraft of Lt. Cd. Haegelen, Bourges, May 1940.
Joanne coll.

Opposite page, bottom:
Aircraft of GC I/2. Photo was taken in July 1940. In the foreground is MS 406 no. 946 flown by Polish pilot por. J. Brzeziński.
De Chasteigner coll. via B. Philippe.

Fighters ... 69

Bloch MB 151 no 370 of GC III/10 in flight.
SHAA

Right:
Bloch MB 152 of GC II/1 destroyed on 15 May 1940 at Couvron airfield.
T. Kopański coll.

Right:
Bloch MB 152 aircraft of GC II/1 probably at Valensole airfield.
SHAA

L'Armée de L'Air Fighters

Bloch MB 152 of GC I/1.
SHAA

Left:
Curtis Hawk 75A, destroyed on the ground.
B. Belcarz coll.

Below:
MB 152, photo was taken at Chantilly Les Aigles airfield.
SHAA

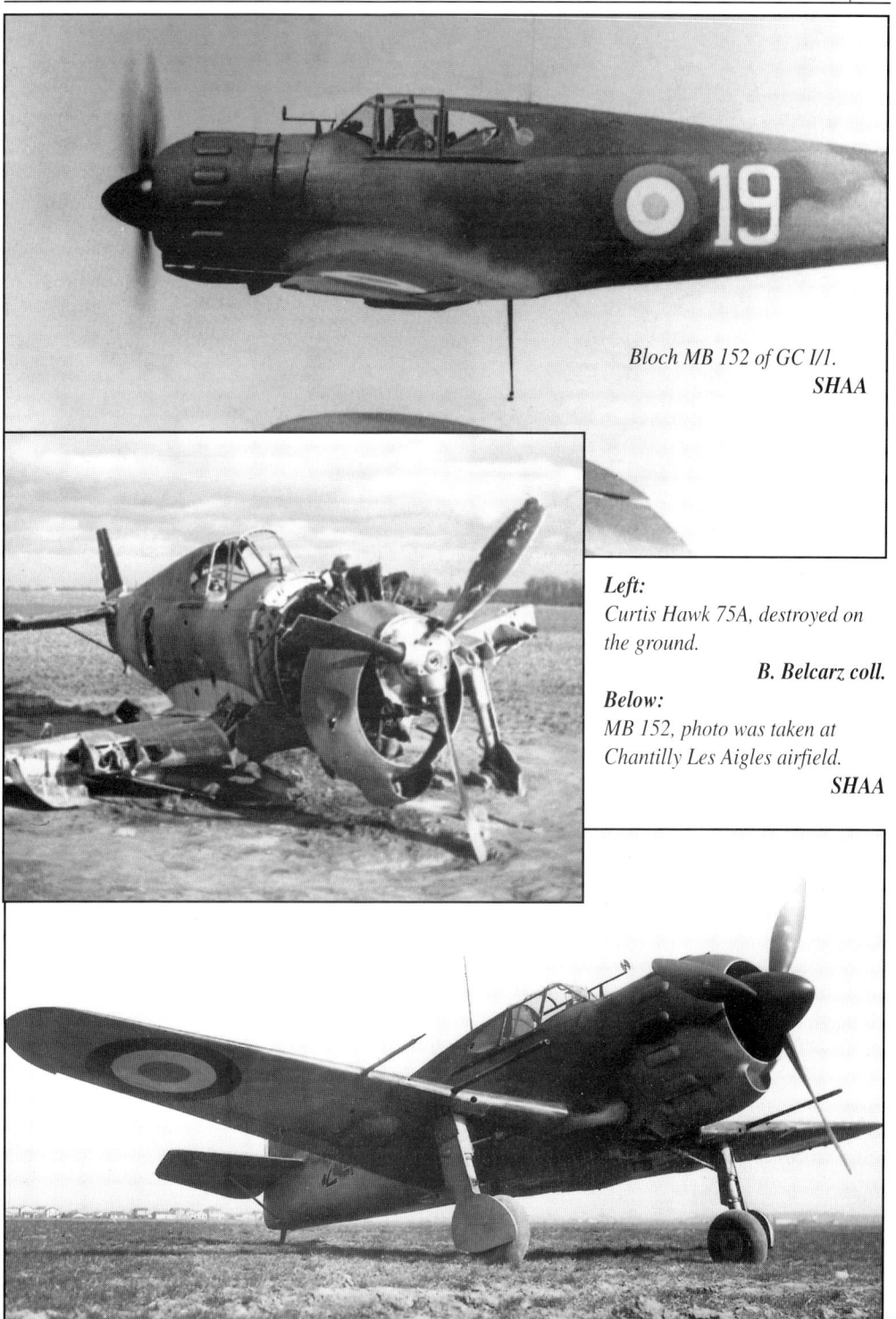

Fighters ... 71

Arsenal VG 33 no. 7 at Toulouse airfield.
SHAA

Above:
Bloch MB 152 at Angers airfield.
SHAA

Right:
Bloch MB 152 destroyed on the ground.
T. Kopański coll.

L'Armée de L'Air Fighters

Above:
D 520 at Toulouse-Francazal Air Base. Photo is dated 28 June 1940.
SHAA

Left:
MS 406s of 4 Esc. GC II/2 (probably) at Mions airfield.
SHAA

Left:
Curtis Hawk 75A of GC II/5 at Mions airfield, 16 June 1940.
K. Chołoniewski coll.

Map of the final German advance.
Map was originally published in "Wehrmachtberichte Weltgeschichte, Der Krieg 1939/40" by Verlag Die Wehrmacht K. G., Berlin, 1941

Jagdwaffe in France
by Robert Michulec

The Germans earmarked two Luftflotten against the Allied might: nos. 2 and 3. These included over 4,500 combat and transport aircraft in total, an extraordinary number in those days. Such vast concentration of force allowed the Germans to swiftly achieve the necessary air superiority. This was possible mainly thanks to the principle of concentration of effort in selected directions, and to the excellent fighting skills of the Jagdwaffe, Göring's pride.

There is no doubt that the German fighter aviation was at that time the best air-fighting formation in the world, and Göring could rightfully boast of his "eagles" as the showcase of the entire Luftwaffe. As of 10 May 1940 the Luftwaffe had no less than 13 fighter and 5 destroyer Geschwadern, obviously impressing foreign analysts. According to contemporary ideas that should have made almost 2,000 aircraft, an admirable force. The reality was less glamorous, though. Although the Germans had 18 Geschwadern of single- and twin-engined fighters, this was only in theory. Many were still in the early stages of forming, so some were in fact little more than "number plates". Some Geschwadern had only a single Gruppe and did not even have separate HQs. Therefore, it would be erroneous to consider them

Bf 109 E-3 of I./JG77 in the first days of May, 1940. Aircraft in 71/02/65 camouflage.

via R. Pęczkowski

Robert Michulec

Military Exhibition in Berlin, early autumn 1940. Bf 109E shown in very striking pose. Aircraft still in the old camouflage used in 1939.

CAW via R. Michulec

full-blooded formations. Without organisational and tactical support from fully established Geschwadern, some of the single- or two-Gruppe units would not be able to exist at all. In consequence, early May 1940 saw the formation of a number of peculiar ad hoc Geschwadern, their teamwork leaving much to be desired. This is well shown with the example of the units based on Stab/JG 27, which on 10 May controlled the following Gruppen: I/JG 21, I/JG 1, I/JG 51 and I/JG 27. On the other hand, II/JG 27 was initially reporting to another Geschwader, while Stab/JG 51 controlled I/JG 26 and I/JG 20.

The Germans were fully aware of the organisational chaos, and the inability to deploy the Jagdwaffe according to their original plans. As a result, during the victorious demobilisation, as soon as the French campaign was over, they started mass re-organisation of their Geschwadern.

Some unit numbers disappeared from the orders of battle, but the strength of the Jagdwaffe remained unchanged. This is how the problem was dealt with:

S, I/JG 1	– disbanded, I Gr re-formed into III/JG 27 in July 1940
S, I, II, III, IV(N)/JG 2	– IV Gr re-formed into II/NJG 1 in June 1940
S, I, II, III/JG	
3 I/JG 20	– re-formed into III/JG 51 in July 1940
I/JG 21	– re-formed into III/JG 54 in July 1940
S, I, II, III/JG 26	
S, I, II/JG 27	
S, I, II, III/JG 51	
S, I, II, III/JG 52	
S, I, II, III/JG 53	
S, I/JG 54 I/JG 76	– re-formed into II/JG 54 in July 1940
S, I, II/JG 77	– I Gr re-formed into IV/JG 51 in August 1940
II(J)/TrGr 186	– re-formed into III/JG 77 in July 1940
I(J)/LG 2	– re-formed into I/JG 77 w 1942
I, II/ZG 1	– disbanded, II Gr into III/ZG 76 in August 1940
S, I/ZG 2	
S, I, II, III/ZG 26	
I/ZG 52	– re-formed into II/ZG 2 in July 1940
S, I, II/ZG 76	
V(Z)/LG 1	– re-formed into I/NJG 3 in the autumn

The above listing shows clearly that the summer of 1940 saw the disbanding of no less than 6 Geschwadern, their components re-formed

76 Fighters ...

Warming up a Bf 109 E-1.
R. Michulec coll.

into additional Gruppen of existing ones. This allowed JG 27, 54 and 77 to reach their full establishment strength, and the JG 51 became the only four-Gruppe Geschwader of the Luftwaffe.

Meanwhile, in late April and early May, the majority of these units were concentrated along the western border of Germany, to fight the French-British alliance, supported by "neutral" Belgium and Holland. The concentration of fighters (and other forces) was possible thanks to several factors. In the spring of 1940 Germany had no other enemies, and there was no possibility of the eastern border suddenly becoming ablaze. Moreover, the French and British were conducting a very passive war, without even trying to stretch the German air defences over the northern coast of the Third

Bf 109E, WNr 1304, white 1 of I./JG 76. Personal aircraft of Fw. Karl Hiera, who landed on French territory after one of the battles at the end of 1939.
This aircraft was tested by the French and later was sent to the UK.
J. Crow coll.

Briefing before next mission, France 1940. One of the speakers is (probably) Oblt. G. Specht of I./ZG 26, with two kills as seen on the Bf 110 (U8+HH) in the foreground.

CAW

Reich. As a result, the Germans encountered no problems concentrating their fighter units on the Rhine and on the Dutch border. Altogether 36 fighter and destroyer Gruppen were assembled there, totalling slightly over 1,600 aircraft. These included almost 1,250 Bf 109Es and over 300 Bf 110s, and also – somewhat in reserve – over 30 Jumo 210-powered Bf 109s (C & D models), and even more than 35 Ar 68s. Thus, in spite of all imperfections and difficulties, this was an impressive force, not just by its numbers, but also because the adversaries could not counter it with an equal mass of similarly good aeroplanes.

Concentration of the Jagdwaffe forces was influenced by an important factor, assured by the high command already during early 1940: reinforcement of unit establishment with extra aircraft. This allowed Gruppen, nominally numbering 40 aircraft, to have in some cases as many as 45-47 machines. Thus, regardless of engine problems, the numbers of serviceable Messerschmitts were as high as 35. This in turn allowed many Gruppen to be ready for maximum combat effort on 10 May. Of course, there were exceptions to this rule, in some cases quite astonishing. In many "Emil" batches the excessive number of engineering problems proved paralysing for some units, allowing them to employ only half of the stipulated Gruppe strength. For example, III/JG 26 "Schlageter" had only 22 serviceable "Emils", or 50% of the establishment!

The Germans deployed almost all they had for the attack against France. The only exceptions were II/JG 77, based in Norway, and Stab and II/JG 3 still based in the Third Reich in mid-May. Equipment and numbers of the earmarked units on the morning of 10 May 1940 were as follows:

Including a single unserviceable Bf 109C

Luftflotte 2

S/JG 1	4/4 Bf 109E	Jever
I	46/24 Bf 109E	Gymnich
II/JG 2	47/35 Bf 109E	Nordholz
IV	31/30 Bf 109D	Hopsten
	36/13 Ar 68	
III/JG 3	37/25 Bf 109E	Hopsten
I/JG 20	48/36 Bf 109E	Bönninghardt
I/JG 21	46/34 Bf 109E	Mönchengladbach
S/JG 26	4/3 Bf 109E	Dortmund
I	44/35 Bf 109E	Bönninghardt
II	47/36 Bf 109E	Dortmund
III	42/22 Bf 109E	Essen-Mühlheim
S/JG 27	4/4 Bf 109E	Mönchengladbach
I	39/28 Bf 109E	Bönninghardt
II	44/34 Bf 109E*	Bönninghardt
S/JG 51	4/3 Bf 109E	Bönninghardt
I/JG 51	47/38 Bf 109E	Krefeld
II(J)/186	48/35 Bf 109E	Wangerooge
I(J)/LG 2	48/32 Bf 109E	Wyk-auf-Föhr/Esbjerg
I/ZG 1	35/22 Bf 110C/D	Kirchenhellen
II/ZG 1	36/26 Bf 110C/D	Gelsenkirchen-Buer
S/ZG 26	3/3 Bf 110C/D	Dortmund
I	32/11 Bf 110C/D	Niedermendig
II	37/30 Bf 110C/D	Krefeld

Bf 110C of 4/ZG 26 with C code letter in flight over France, spring 1940. Zerstörer units had heavy losses during the French campaign, almost equal to their victories.
CAW via R. Michulec

Robert Michulec

A Schwarm of Bf 110s, probably of ZG 26, in flight summer 1940.
CAW

The HQ of Lfe 2 controlled 666 fighters and 145 destroyers. However, only 72% of the fighters and 57% of the destroyers were serviceable, poor figures under those conditions (short supply lines, long time for preparations, units in permanent bases...). As a result, instead of 842 machines, only 582 aircraft were serviceable, including 500 single-engined ones. The true number was 539, though, including 457 Bf 109Es, as the Jumo-powered Messerschmitts and the Arados were completely useless in those days of May 1940.

Another Bf 109 E-3 of I./JG77 in May 1940.
via R. Pęczkowski

80 Fighters ...

Luftflotte 3

Unit	Strength/Aircraft	Base
S/JG 2	4/4 Bf 109E	Frankfurt-Rebstock
I	45/33 Bf 109E	Frankfurt-Rebstock
III	42/11 Bf 109E	Frankfurt-Rebstock
I/JG 3	48/38 Bf 109E	Vogelsang
II/JG 51	42/30 Bf 109E	Böblingen
S/JG 52	3/3 Bf 109E	Mannheim-Sandhofen
I	46/33 Bf 109E	Lachen/Speyerdorf
II	42/28 Bf 109E	Speyer
III	48/39 Bf 109E	Mannheim-Sandhofen
S/JG 53	4/4 Bf 109E	Wiesbaden-Erbenheim
I	46/33 Bf 109E	Wiesbaden-Erbenheim
II	45/37 Bf 109E	Wiesbaden-Erbenheim
III	44/33 Bf 109E	Wiesbaden-Erbenheim
S/JG 54	4/4 Bf 109E	Böblingen
I/JG 54	42/27 Bf 109E	Böblingen
I/JG 76	46/39 Bf 109E	Ober-Olm
S/JG 77	4/3 Bf 109E	Peppenhoven
I	46/28 Bf 109E	Odendorf
S/ZG 2	3/2 Bf 110C/D	Darmstadt-Griesheim
I	32/22 Bf 110C/D	Darmstadt-Griesheim
II/ZG 26	35/25 Bf 110C/D	Kaarst/Neuss
I/ZG 52	35/23 Bf 110C/D	Neuhausen ob Eck
S/ZG 76	3/3 Bf 110C/D	Cologne-Wahn
II/ZG 76	33/25 Bf 110C/D	Cologne-Wahn
V(S)/LG 1	33/27 Bf 110C/D	Mannheim-Sandhofen

Bf 109 E of I./JG 27, ready for combat missions, late autumn, 1939. Aircraft still in old type camouflage which was changed in the next few months.
Petrick via R. Michulec

The HQ of Lfe 3 had 601 fighters and 174 destroyers. As with Lfe 2, this formation had a relatively low percentage of serviceable aircraft: only 71% of fighters and 73% of destroyers. Thus, only 554 aircraft out of 775 were ready for use, including 427 single-seat Messerschmitts.

To sum up: the Germans were able to use against their enemies 1,298 fighters and 319 destroyers, of which 927 and 209, respectively, were serviceable (1,136 in total).

This was much more than the French and British, but the numbers were not all. What really mattered was the quality of the Jagdwaffe fighters. The force was based on two aircraft types: Bf 109E and Bf 110C. For their time, both were almost perfect from the tactical and engineering viewpoints, and would have no equals over France until late May 1940, when RAF Spitfires joined in the fighting. Even the latest AdA fighter type, the Dewoitine D.520, could not quite match the single-engined Messerschmitt, although it was equal to the twin-engined machine in most respects.

Both German designs achieved 560-540 km/h at an altitude of 6,000 m, where they were barely accessible to their opponents, as most fighters of the other side were optimised for operations at an altitude of 4,000-5,000 m. This gave German pilots an important advantage over the enemy, increased by the better tactics employed by the Germans. Both the French and the British were rather passive in their actions, whilst German fighters were always aggressive and very flexible. Another advantage, perhaps even more important than the other ones, was the high morale of German pilots who felt superior and were eager to engage the enemy. This, and the initiative that belonged to the Germans once they started their invasion, provided an important psychological boost that put them at an advantage with regard to their opponents.

Close up view of Bf 109 E undercarriage. Photo was taken at one of the Luftwaffe air bases in the spring of 1940.
CAW

Cockpit of Bf 110 C.
via R. Pęczkowski

The German offensive commenced with an attack against Holland and Belgium, within the Luftflotte 2 area of operations. It was there that the heaviest combats were fought initially. Although the defenders failed to mount any major actions during the first days of fighting, it suffered, nevertheless, serious losses that can be estimated at 40-50 aircraft per day.

Fighting over the German border immediately became fierce and bloody. From the very beginning the Germans were better than their adversaries, be they Dutch, Belgian (their forces being virtually annihilated the first day), French, or British. In the case of the Dutch and Belgians the advantage resulted mainly from the element of surprise which made it possible to destroy their air forces on the ground. Whatever was left of them, was so small in numbers that they could not affect the battle, heavily outnumbered by the Germans. What the encounters could have looked like, had the Dutch more forces, is well illustrated by the combat of II(J)/TrGr 186 and 1 JaVa. During a fierce 10 minute encounter the Germans were able to destroy just one Fokker D.XXI, losing two of their Bf 109s. Combats with other Dutch fighter units were similar. For example, during the interception of a Dutch bombing raid which included seven D.XXIs of 2 JaVa, the Germans of 6/JG 27 were only able to shoot down a single fighter for no loss. This shows that Dutch fighters were tough opponents for the Germans, clearly standing out as compared to other enemies of the Jagdwaffe.

Bf 109 E-3 (or E-4) of 2./JG 21, spring 1940.

CAW

Bf 109 E fighters of I/JG 3 at one of the German bases, spring 1940. Aircraft in typical camouflage of that period.

CAW

Constant fighting during the first day of the real war resulted in strongly varying victory/loss returns: over 50 allied aircraft shot down for just 9 Luftwaffe fighters destroyed from all causes. OKW reports for that day mentioned a mere 23 air victories, while German fighters claimed no less than 80 kills. In reality they destroyed over 60 aircraft: approximately 10 each Dutch and Belgian ones, no less than 13 French and almost 30 British.

Allied losses in the air amounted to 38 RAF machines, 14 AdA aircraft, and some 20 Dutch and Belgian ones, 72 aircraft in total. German losses amounted to 106 combat aircraft, plus no less than 66 Ju 52s.

A further peak of enemy losses and German successes came on 12 May, during the fighting over the Maastricht crossings, and then on 14 May, when the Allies attempted to destroy the bridges at Sedan.

In the former case the Germans claimed a total of 58 victories, of which 20 were credited to pilots reporting to Stab/JG 27, i. e. 2/JG 27 and 2/JG 1, who achieved 15 kills. During fierce fighting against Hurricanes, Battles, and Blenheims, Oblt. G. Framm and Oblt. W. Adolph claimed 3 victories each, the day's best individual scores. The same battle saw the beginning of Adolf Galland's bright career, when he claimed 2 Hurricanes shot down. He would go on to score 12 more victories, including five over fighters. The first 12 kills achieved while in JG 27 made no less than 2/3 of the total number of victories scored by the Stab/JG 27 during fighting over France.

In the other case, a similar battle was fought on a greater scale. British bombers were decimated on 14 May at Sedan. According to the OKW announcement, the Germans claimed 170 enemy aircraft shot down, but the source for this number is not known. Available data prove that German airmen claimed some 100 victories that day, mostly over Sedan. I/JG 53 distinguished itself with 39 claims, of which five were by Oblt. H. K. Mayer. He shot down two Battles, two Blenheims and a Hurricane. Second to JG 53 "Pik-As", JG 2 "Richthofen" also achieved a respectable success, claiming 20 aircraft according to the unit records, including eight between 8.00 and 8.30 p.m. These included two slow Amiot 143s of GB I/34 and II/34, first targeted by Flak, and then finished off by III/JG 2 pilots.

On 14 May the Germans did not content themselves with bomber formations. Jagdflieger taught a painful lesson to a French fighter unit, butchered by I/JG 3 at Dinant after 8.00 p.m. According to German reports, 7-8 H-75 fighters were downed, but in reality they almost certainly bounced GC II/1 which lost five MB.152s that day. Pilots of the German unit proved their ability on 17 May, when they encountered a formation of twelve 82 Squadron Blenheims at St Quentin and blew them out of the sky. The Germans considered all the RAF bombers shot down, but the British unit lost 11 aircraft destroyed and one damaged (victories were claimed by just 5 German pilots). Three of the victims were credited to Lt. Sprenger, and no less than four to Lt. M. Buchholz, who added two more victories at midday. This made Buchholz the most outstanding Jagdwaffe ace of the campaign, his record remaining unbeaten.

The same day saw the decimation of French bombers by I/JG 2, and more precisely by 6 pilots of 2 and 3 Staffeln. Those fighters claimed

Bf 110 C of 1./ZG1, spring 1940.

CAW

Bf 109 E fighters of III./JG 53 ready to take off. Winter 1939/40. Note that noses are in different colours, an effect of the new type of camouflage based on RLM 71/02 colours.

CAW

destruction of seven LeO 451s out of 26 encountered, but in fact GB I/34 and GB II/12 lost only 4 bombers destroyed, including – according to French records – two to ground fire. Perhaps the French data are more reliable, as the victories included three by Lt. H. Wick who was not known for particular accuracy in his claims during WW2. Similar overclaiming happened the following day when a group of pilots of the same 3/JG 2 encountered six Blenheims of no. 15 Squadron. The Germans claimed 6 kills, while the British lost 4 bombers, including one that returned safely, but was declared damaged beyond repair.

That 17th May combat was not the only one when I/JG 2 pilots encountered night bombers of the AdA. The "Richthofen" pilots seemed to have particular attraction to LeO aircraft. On 20 May they encountered GB I, GB II/12 and GB I/31 machines again, and claimed eight (including seven in one minute!), but in fact they destroyed four out of ten participating in the action. Wick accounted for a couple again. On 31 May 2 Staffel pilots claimed seven LeOs destroyed – GB I/11, GB I/12, GB I/31, GB II/31 – while another one was downed by II/JG 3. In fact these units lost 13 bombers out of 20 that participated in the operation.

Another peak in kill numbers came over Dunkirk during late May, and then in the Paris area on 3 and 5 June. It was then that the Germans eliminated the last signs of organised resistance over Central France, with more overclaiming than at the beginning of the "Fall Gelb". For example, on 3 June they claimed 79 victories, while the French lost 17 aircraft, and the British six; a total of a mere 23 machines, not counting the damaged ones.

It was similar on 5 June, when the Germans claimed 49 aircraft, but in fact they destroyed no less than 32 AdA machines, at least according to French records.

Similar successes were achieved on 6 and 9 June, when the Germans supposedly shot down 64 and 68 enemy aircraft, respectively. On both these days the French indeed suffered serious losses, but less than the Germans claimed: on 6 June 29 aircraft were destroyed in air combat, and on 9 June 17 aircraft (plus 8 more believed shot down by Flak).

All in all, according to the OKW announcements, during just the main part of the Battle of France ("Fall Gelb"), from 10 May to 3 June (inclusive), the Germans achieved 1,841 aerial victories, of which 1,142 were by fighters, against the Allies. Another 699 aircraft were claimed as shot down by the AA artillery. The data are broken down on a daily basis below:*

Date	Victories	Flak	Losses
10 May	23	3	26
11 May	52	12	35
12 May	58	72	31
13 May	47	37	27
14 May	170	17	35
15 May	46	2	18
16 May	30	8	15
17 May	53	11	26
18 May	47	13	27
19 May	95	15	31
20 May	47	?	?
21 May	35	14	10
22 May**	?	?	5

Source: Dr Erich Murawski - Der Durchbruch im Westen - Gerhard Stalling Verlagsbuchhandlung, 1940.

*** That day the Germans claimed 9 enemy aircraft destroyed in air combats and by ground fire.*

Bf 109 E-3, W.Nr 5102 of I./JG 77 Gruppen Adjutant. Aircraft with personal emblem and name "Kieki". See also colour profile on page 144.

Budesarchiv

Robert Michulec

* That day the Germans claimed 3 enemy aircraft destroyed in air combats and by ground fire.

** By 4 June 1,841 including 1,142 for the fighters; after 3 June another 383 victories, without victor details. The OKW considered these 383 victories as achieved solely by fighters, hence the number of 1,525 kills.
In reality the OKW numbers differ from actual data, although it is not known why and how much. We know that the data for 10 May was reduced by half while those for 14 May overclaimed by some 100%.

23 May	25	8	16
24 May	27	14	7
25 May	19	17	11
26 May	32	15	15
27 May	63	11	23
28 May	16	8	3
29 May	68	17	15
30 May*	?	?	2
31 May	39	10	9
1 June	42	15	8
2 June	27	15	10
3 June	79	9	21

In total the Germans considered that from 10 May to 22 June they shot down some 2,224* aircraft in air combats, including some 1,525 by fighters. Additionally, the German Flak was credited with 854 enemy machines shot down.

Losses of the Jagdwaffe and Zerstörerwaffe in France can be estimated at over 200 aircraft. During the entire period of May and June, 169 Bf 109 and 90 Bf 110 aircraft were struck off charge as destroyed, a total of 259 aircraft.

Available daily returns of the RLM show that during operations from 10 May to 23 June the Germans lost 244 Bf 109s and 110 Bf 110s damaged (presumably seriously) or destroyed. The differences are therefore not great, and especially considering that pilots of these units certainly shot down some 1,000 aircraft, their operations have to be seen as an outstanding success.

Generally, the victory-to-loss ratio was by all measures favourable for the Jagdwaffe. For example, JG 3 claimed 181 kills for the loss of 32 Bf 109s in combat. Similarly, JG 27 claimed 218 victories for almost 45 Messerschmitts lost.

Another view of the Bf 109 E-3 "Kieki". Aircraft in typical "France" camouflage RLM71/02/65.
Bundesarchiv

88 Fighters ...

Aircraft of I./JG 77 at Odendorf airfield just before the French Campaign. Note the gun outlets in a different colour (yellow ?)
Bundesarchiw

JG 27 proved the most successful fighter Geschwader of the Luftwaffe, and its **Oblt. Balthasar**, 1/JG 1 commander, was the most successful fighter pilot of the Battle of France.

Wilhelm Balthasar displayed his skills already on the second day of the war when he led his 1 Staffel into action over Belgium, where he encountered Gladiators of the Belgian 1 Escadrille. The 15 minute combat resulted in the defeat of the Belgians, and 6 of the biplanes shot down, three by the German ace. It seems certain that the commander of the Belgian unit, Capt. M. Guisgand, was one of the victims of Balthasar.

This success was repeated by Balthasar on 23 May over Douai, when his unit bounced British Hurricanes and during a 30 minute combat his pilots again claimed 6 aircraft shot down, including three again by the German ace himself. One of these was his 10th kill. His victories reach a peak on 5 June, when he managed to down 5 enemy aircraft in two actions. During the first one he managed to down three French bombers, and then two fighters, also French. But that was not the end of Balthasar's spectacular successes over France, as the following day he led his Staffel against an enemy bomber formation. During a prolonged combat the Germans claimed over 20 victories, of which no less than four were credited to the 1/JG 1 commander, the largest single success in his fighter career.

His outstanding record was mentioned in the OKW announcement of 14 June which informed that on 13 June he was awarded the Knight's Cross for shooting down his 20th enemy aircraft by 7 June. This was the second such mention; as early as 29 May the OKW announced that Mölders had achieved that mark.

Robert Michulec

Bf 109 E of II./JG 51, France 1940. Note rather unusual camouflage, but typical for this unit.
Petrick via R. Michulec

With the end of the fighting in France Balthasar had 23 kills to his credit, scored between 10 May and 13 June, almost within a month! These victories accounted for no less than 62% of the total number of kills of his 1 Staffel, and also 28% of the kill total of I/JG 1 led by Hptm. Schlichting. It was also the best result achieved by a German fighter pilot. The scoreboard of this ace of the Battle of France is as follows:

Date	Aircraft	No.	Time	Area
11 May	Gladiator	1	06:55	Maastricht area
	Gladiator	2	06:5?	Maastricht area
	Gladiator	3	06:58	Maastricht area
11 May	MS.406	4	19:51	Maastricht area
13 May	Hurricane	5	06:15	Jodoigne
17 May	H-75	6	13:55	Compiegne
19 May	Lysander	7	13:50	Amiens
23 May	Hurricane	8	14:10	Douai
	Hurricane	9	14:20	Douai
	Hurricane	10	14:20	Douai
26 May	Spitfire	11	09:45(?)	Calais area
	Spitfire	12	10:03	Calais area
5 June	LeO 451	13	10:40	Montdidier
	Potez 63	14	10:48	Nesle
	LeO 451	15	10:50	Nesle
	MS.406	16	21:20	Roye
	MS.406	17	21:30	Roye

90 Fighters ...

6 June	MS.406	18	16:40	Roye	
	LeO 451	19	16:50	Roye	
	LeO 451	20	16:55	Roye	
	LeO 451	21	17:05	Ham	
13 June	Potez 63	22	17:50	Provins	
	Blenheim	23	18:20	Sezanne	

The above listing shows clearly that Balthasar would seldom return from a sortie with a single kill. What is more, his scoreboard - and thus also the kill markings on the fin of his mount - included eleven machines destroyed on the ground while strafing French and Belgian airfields. But, even more importantly, Balthasar was never shot down, and his Messerschmitt was never even damaged! It is all this information put together that really shows the class of the pilot.

Many other pilots of the Jagdwaffe displayed similar high skills. JG 27 had Oblt. G. Homuth and Oblt. G. Framm, each with a total of 9 victories, the same number as the score of Hptm. G. Lützow of JG 3.

A similar number of kills was also scored by Lts. von Hahn (JG 53), Sprick and Müncheberg (JG 26), and Rudorffer (JG 2), and by Hptm. Gentzen (ZG 2). Better results were achieved by Oblt. Mayer (JG 53) and Lt. Machold (JG 2), each with 10 victories, and by the legendary Wick and Galland: the former with 12, and the latter with 14 kills. One more victory was scored by Mölders.

Bf 109 of I./JG 27 and Ju 87 of III./StG2 at Ochamps airfield.
P. Taghon coll.

Above:
Bf 110C of ZG 26 "Horst Wessel"
SHAA

Right:
Bf 110C of Erg ZG over Paris.
Stratus coll.

Below:
Bf 109 of II./JG 27 at Wesel-West, 10.05.1940.
P. Taghon coll.

Fighters of the Luftwaffe

Above:
Fw. Emil Clade I./JG 1 at Gymnich airfield.

Left:
Bf 109, Hs 126 and wrecked Potez at Charleville airfield.

Gymnich 12.05.1940,
From left:
Hptm Balthasar,
Oblt. Kirstein,
Obt. Adolph,
Hptm. Schlichting.
All photos P. Taghon coll.

Fighters ... 93

Robert Michulec

Bf 109 of Ofw. Walter Grimmling, 1./JG 53, crashed near Bouillon on 14.05.1940.
P. Taghon coll.

Right:
Bf 109 of II./TrG 186 in May 1940.
P. Taghon coll.

Below:
Bf 110 C of 5./ZG 26.
SHAA

94 Fighters ...

Fighters of the Luftwaffe

Above: *Bf 109 E, W. Nr. 3326 captured by Lt. Mercier on 25 September 1939.*

Left: *Bf 110 of 5./ZG 26 in France, June 1940.*

Both photos SHAA

Bf 109 E in France 1940. Aircraft undergoing major repairs.

SHAA

Fighters ... 95

Above: Bf 109 E-3 of 4./JG53, spring 1940, French-German border. Personal aircraft of Staffelkapitan (commander) pf 4./JG53, Hptm. H. Kroeck. Note the mirror on the canopy, very often mounted on Emils during the French Campaign.

Stratus coll.

Below: Bf 109 E-3 of 6./JG53, France 1940, in readiness. Aircraft in typical camouflage of that period. Aircraft also fitted with mirror on the canopy.

Stratus coll.

Polish Air Force Fighters in France
by Bartłomiej Belcarz

The Polish Air Force fought in France within the Armée de l'Air. The agreement signed between France and Poland on 4 January 1940 said that:

"Polish air units will be used by the French high command under the same conditions as the French air force, while maintaining their allied air force status".

The agreement laid formal ground for establishment of Polish air units in France, and thus for commencement of training. Only fighter pilots achieved combat readiness during the 1940 campaign. Their experience, gained during the defence of Poland in 1939, proved extremely useful here.

The first to achieve operational status was one of the flights of the planned II Fighter Squadron (under Maj. M. Mümler). It was known informally as the "Montpellier Flight", as its initial training took place at that base. This lasted from 7 January until 15 February 1940. Upon its completion the Poles returned to Lyon-Bron, the main base of the Polish Air Force in France.

Results of the training were appreciated so highly by the French superiors, that its time frame was cut short. This led to consternation at Lyon, where nobody expected the "Montpellier Flight" to return so soon, as the course had been planned to end in mid-March 1940. The problem was solved by sending the pilots away on leave. Once they returned, a propaganda ceremony was stage to celebrate the fact that the Polish Air Force was ready to fight again.

On 27 March 1940, in the presence of the highest French and Polish military officials, the 18 Polish pilots, divided into three-aircraft sections, were assigned to French units for operational practice. Upon its completion, it was planned, they would return to form a Polish fighter squadron. As it turned out, this never happened. Individual sections were allocated as follows:

Mjr Józef Kępiński, the commander of GC 1/145.
Pawlak coll.

Section	Officer commanding	GC allocation	Base
Section no. 1	Capt. S. Łaszkiewicz	GC III/2	Cambrai
Section no. 2	Capt. J. Pentz	GC II/6	Anglure
Section no. 3	Capt. M. Sulerzycki	GC III/6	Wez-Thiusy
Section no. 4	Lt. K. Bursztyn	GC III/1	Toul Croix de Metz
Section no. 5	Lt. J. Brzeziński	GC I/2	Xaffevillers
Section no. 6	Lt. W. Goettel	GC II/7	Luxeuil

Some of these sections were later joined by more Polish pilots, but this was after hostilities started in earnest, when French activities were a question of chance rather than choice.

While the "Montpellier Flight" was still under training, another fighter squadron started to form. In the Polish nomenclature this was III Fighter

Above: Gen. Sikorski raising the Polish flag at Lyon-Bron air base. Potez 63-11 is seen in the background.
Pi&SM

Below: Offical celebrations just before departure of the first Polish fighter unit to the front.
B. Belcarz coll.

Squadron, commanded by Maj. J. Kępiński. It underwent its training, similar to I Fighter Squadron (under Lt. Col. L. Pamuła) at Lyon-Bron. A faster pace of training of III Fighter Squadron resulted from the fact that it was formed from pilots who volunteered for the fighter unit to be sent to Finland, invaded by the USSR. The number of volunteers, no less than 150, far exceeded the standard number of 30 pilots in a squadron. It was planned that the Squadron would be equipped with Caudron C.714s, as Finland had purchased a number of these aeroplanes in France. The armistice in the Winter War was signed during training, leading to a change of plans with regard to the unit which would be retained in France. On 6 April 1940 Gen. Picard signed the orders that gave III Fighter Squadron its official French number of GC 1/145. At the request of the Poles, the unit was named "Varsovie" ("Warsaw"). The start of operations found GC 1/145 still at Lyon-Bron. For the first week the squadron aircraft (at that time still MS 406s of the Polish Air Force Training

Combat effort of GC 1/145 between 10 May and 19 June 1940

Base	Period	Number of missions	Number of sorties	Total flying hours	Mission type
Lyon - Bron	10.05.40	3	9	9	air defence of Lyon and Bron aerodrome
Lyon - Mions	10.05.- 18.05.40	6	16	19	air defence of Lyon and Mions aerodrome
Villacoublay	20.05.- 2.06.40	23	86	92	air defence of Villacoublay and the aerodrome
Dreux - Maison La Blanche	3.06. - 10.06.40	19	161	188	14 combat missions 5 missions air defence of Dreux and the base
Sermaises	11.06.- 13.06.40	2	6	6	air defence of the area
Châteauroux	14.06.- 17.06.40	7	34	34	air defence of the area
Rochefort	17.06.- 19.06.40	4	10	10	3 missions air defence of the area 1 reconnaissance mission
Total		64	322	358	

MS 406s of the French unit arrived to attend the official celebration at Lyon-Bron (27 March 1940). Nose of MS 406 no 1031, the personal aircraft of por. Bursztyn, in the foreground.

SHAA

Centre [DIAP] at Lyon, as the unit had only four C.714s) defended the city and the base. On 18 May 1940 the unit moved to Villacoublay.

During late May 1940 the squadron was visited by the French Minister of Aviation, Guy de Chambre, who grounded the C.714s upon learning of their faults (which had caused many failures and several accidents). However, due to lack of any other equipment, the Poles continued to fly them, on their own responsibility. During the fighting, on 10 June, the squadron OC, Maj. J. Kępiński was severely wounded in combat with a Bf 109. He was replaced by Capt. P. Laguna, who then commanded the squadron until its evacuation from France. During the combat operations, two officers from the base at Lyon were posted to the unit: Col. S. Pawlikowski and A. L. de Marmier. At the end of the campaign GC 1/145 received its first Bloch 151 aircraft, which were planned to requip the unit, but this proved too late. During fighting the pilots of GC 1/145 achieved the following victories:

no.	Date	Pilot	Area	Aircraft type	Category	Notes
1	8.06.1940	Capt. A. Wczelik Lt. T. Czerwiński	Aumale	Do 17	Confirmed 1	I/KG 76 Do 17
2	9.06.1940	2Lt. Cz. Główczyński	Les Andelys	Bf 109	Confirmed 1	II/JG 27
3	9.06.1940	2Lt. J. Czerniak	Les Andelys	Bf 109	Confirmed 1	II/JG 27
4	9.06.1940	Cpl M. Parafiński	Louviers	Bf 109	Confirmed 1	II/JG 27
5	9.06.1940	Capt. A. Wczelik Lt. J. Kowalski Cpl A. Markiewicz	Louviers	Do 17	Confirmed 1	
6	10.06.1940	2Lt. J. Czerniak	North of Dreux	Do 17	Confirmed 1	
7	10.06.1940	2Lt. A. Żukowski	North of Dreux	Do 17	Confirmed 1	
8	10.06.1940	Capt. P. Łaguna	Henouville	Bf 109	Confirmed 1	

These were paid for by 3 dead and 2 wounded.

MS 406, no. 939 abandoned by GC III/2 at Cambrai Airfield.
P. Taghon coll.

After the German attack, there was still a large group of Polish fighters at Lyon. They were the pilots who were intended to form the I and IV Fighter Squadrons, as well as the II Flight of the II Squadron (the I Flight was already fighting as the "Montpellier Flight"). Rapid and deterioration of the situation at the front line made it unrealistic to form purely Polish units of them, similar to the GC 1/145. As they still presented a significant potential, it was decided to use them to fill in gaps in front-line units, and to form special territorial defence sections, known as DAT sections, to defend important military objects. Apart from that, a Polish training fighter flight (under Mjr M. Wiórkiewicz) was based at Lyon-Bron, and then at St. Symphorien d'Ozon (Mions), and this constituted an element of air defence in Lyon-St Etienne area after the GC 1/145 moved to the front line.

Front-line sections assigned to French fighter squadrons.

Front-line sections	Unit	Date when sent for operations	Number of pilots	Victories	Losses (killed)
Barański section	GC III/6	8.06.1940	3	-	-
Cebrzyński section	GC II/6	18.05.1940	3	2″ + 1	-
Gabszewicz section	GC III/10	2.06.1940	6	-	-
Januszewicz section	GC II/7	18.05.1940	3	1 + 0	-
Jastrzębski section	GC II/1	18.05.1940	6	1 + 1	-
Paszkiewicz section	GC II/8	18.05.1940	3	-	1
Skiba section[1]	GC II/8	7.06.1940	3	-	-
Wczelik section[2]	GC I/1	12.06.1940	8	0 +1	-
Więckowski section	GC III/9	10.06.1940	6	-	-
Wyrwicki section	GC II/10	2.06.1940	6	1 +0	3
Total			47	5″ + 3	4

* Victories listed as (shot down + damaged).

MB 152 no. 622, "Iraś" of 3 Esc. GC II/6. Personal aircraft of plut. Szaposznikow.

S. Joanne coll.

Right:
Kpt. Sulerzycki in the cockpit of his MS 406, Lyon-Bron, 27 March 1940.

B. Belcarz coll.

Right:
A very rare photo of a Bloch 220 mobilised from Air France. In the photo personnel of GC III/6 are ready to move to a new base.

B. Belcarz coll.

Right:
Airmen of 1 Esc. GC III/1. From the left:
Lt. Leenhardt, ppor. Gnys, Sgt. Prolon, ppor. Chciuk, kpt. Legezynski,
Cne. Pampe, por. Bursztyn, Sgt. Carade.
Toul-Croix airfield.

SHAA

Left:
Section no 5 of "Montpellier Squadron" detached to GC I/2. from the left: por. Brzezinski, ppor. Chalupa, plut. Beda. Lyon-Bron, 27 March 1940.
B. Belcarz coll.
Below:
Caudron C 714 on a temporary airfield.
PI&SM

Kpr. Uchto of GC 1/145 with MS 406 no. 901, during training at Lyon-Bron, spring 1940.
Główczynski

While the front-line sections operated within French GCs, the territorial defence DAT sections were left to their own devices. Several names for the DAT sections are used in the literature: ECD (Escadrille de Chasse de Defense – Defence Fighter Flight), ELD (Escadrille Legere de Defense – Light Defence Flight), but also Patrouille de Protection (Protection Section), or Patrouille d'Usine (Factory Section), and even Patrouille de Cheminée (Chimney Section)! Analysis of wartime French documents fails to confirm the nomenclature applied by historians. While the task of the DAT units seems clear, the various nomenclatures seem rather speculative.

Among these units, the largest was that led by Capt. W. Jasionowski, which used Koolhoven FK 58 aircraft. These were Dutch airframes with French engines, and Polish pilots: another aircraft of the French Air Force (apart from the C.714) used virtually solely by the Poles (some aircraft of the type were assigned to French units for training).

Short analysis of the DAT sections reveals that the number of pilots would be sufficient to establish three fighter squadrons (GCs). But in reality, organisation of such units in administrative terms exceeded the capabilities of the French in May 1940. Those sections that left for the front line fulfilled their duty with distinction, as proved by their victory-to-loss ratio of 10.5 : 4. This result is even more impressive, considering that the section commanders would not always find cooperation from their French superiors. Lt. Falkowski, who arrived at Cognac aircraft depot on 31 May 1940, would have to stay there until 15 June before he obtained 5 aircraft, of which only three were serviceable. In such cases the operational activities were a question of statistics rather than reality. The sections of Sałkiewicz and Kosiński fared much better, arriving at aerodromes with stocks of aircraft just manufactured (Dewoitine D.520s at Toulouse) or just assembled (Curtiss H.75A Hawks at Bourges), so that modern equipment was readily available to them.

DAT sections included one which achieved the best result of all Polish units, when compared to the numbers involved: the section of kpt. Opulski that defended Ramorantin, which scored 5 kills for no losses.

DAT territorial defence units and their combat effort during May - June 1940.

DAT territorial defence units	Base	Date	Personnel	Victories / Losses (killed)	Reinforcements
Krasnodębski section GC I/55	Châteaudun Etampes	12.05.1940	6 + 14	-/-	3 + 0
Falkowski section	Cognac	30.05.1940	6 + 24	-/-	2 + 0
Kolubiński section	Rennes	6.03.1940	5 + 0	-/1	-
Kuzian section	Nantes	12.05.1940	4 + 13	-/-	2 + 0
Henneberg section	Châteauroux	12.05.1940	4 + 13	"/-	10 + 0
Janota section	Angers	25.05.1940	6 + 16	-/-	-
Kosiński section	Bourges	16.05.1940	7 + 13	2/-	-
Kowalczyk section	La Rochelle	31.05.1940	6 + 24	-/-	-
Opulski section	Ramorantin	12.05.1940	6 + 15	5/-	2 + 0
Sałkiewicz section	Toulouse	12.05.1940	4 + 13	-/1	4 + 7[1]
Koolhoven Flight	Salon Clermont-Ferrand	24.05.1940	15 + 34	-/1	2 + 0[2]
Fighter Flight of the DIAP Lyon	Lyon-Mions	10.05.1940	12 + 26[3]	3/1	-
Total			**81 + 205**	**10 " /4**	**18 + 7**

* Note that the numbers of personnel should be regarded as provisional.

They partly overlap with other sections (for example, many pilots of the DIAP Lyon Fighter Flight were later posted to front-line units).

Moreover, Poles would voluntarily organise air defence of the bases where they underwent training. In most cases they only had obsolete types of aircraft at their disposal, such as the Dewoitine D.500/510 or Nieuport Delage NiD.621, which stood no chance against modern enemy designs.

Fortunately for those defending Caen, Blida, or Bussac, they did not have to engage the enemy in the air. Poles fighting in French units added 11 enemy aircraft destroyed during the 1940 campaign to the overall score.

While working on the history of the PAF in France I have analysed many documents and publications on the subject. Based on these, I conclude that the successes of the Polish Air Force in France were as follows:
– 34 enemy aircraft shot down individually
– 19 aircraft shot down, shared with French pilots
– 8 aircraft damaged by the Poles
– 3 aircraft shared damaged with French pilots.

The list of Polish top scorers in France is also slightly different in my opinion. On page 108 is my interpretation of these.

Caudron C 714 "13" personal aircraft of por. Aleksy Żukowski of 1 Esc. GC 1/145.
P. Taghon coll.

North American A 57 of Ecole de Pilotage No 1 at Etamps. On this aircraft (no. 39) Polish pilots made training flights.
Wandzilak

Koolhoven FK 58 no 11. Por. Grzeszczak made some combat missions in this aircraft.
Regier via Joanne

106 Fighters ...

FK 58 serial no 17 at Clermont-Ferrand airfield, of DAT Flight commanded by kpt. Jasionowski.

SHAA

Bloch MB 152 (serial no 656). Using this aircraft por. Henneberg escaped to the UK.

Contillion via Aero

MS 406 of DAT Flight at Ramorantin. Personal aircraft of kpt. Opulski. Aircraft crashed during landing after a training flight.

K. Chołoniewski

List of individual scores of Polish Air Force pilots in France in 1940.

Pilot	Victories	Aircraft type		Date	Damaged		Date
ppor. S. Chałupa GC I/2	2 + 2	1	Bf 109	8.06.1940	1/2	Ju 88	11.05.1940
		1	Ju 87	8.06.1940	1	He 111	15.06.1940
		1/3	He 111	2.06.1940			
		1/3	Ju 87	8.06.1940			
ppor. E. Kawnik GC III/6	2 + 0	1	Ju 88	14.05.1940			
		1	Do 17	20.05.1940			
ppor. J. Czerniak GC I/145	2 + 0	1	Bf 109	9.06.1940			
		1	Do 17	10.06.1940			
kpr. E. Nowakiewicz GC II/7	1 + 5	1	Hs 126	14.06.1940	1/2	Do 215	10.06.1940
		1/16	He 111	11.05.1940			
		1/3	He 111	1.06.1940			
		1/3	He 111	4.06.1940			
		1/2	Do 17	14.06.1940			
		1/2	Do 17	15.06.1940			
ppor. W. Król GC II/7	1 + 2	1	Do 17	2.06.1940	1	He 111	24.05.1940
		1/4	He 111	14.05.1940			
		1/5	Do 215	10.06.1940			
por. A. Cebrzyński GC II/6	1 + 2	1	He 111	5.06.1940			
		1/2	He 111	5.06.1940			
		1/3	Hs 126	15.06.1940			
mjr M. Mümler GC II/7	1 + 1	1	He 111	1.06.1940	1	Do 17	15.06.1940
		1/2	Do 17	15.06.1940			
por. M. Trzebiński GC II/1	1 + 1	1	He 111	2.06.1940			
		1/2	Hs 126	10.06.1940			

These victories were paid for by the loss of 14 fighter pilots and 49 aircraft lost in combat or during German attacks against airfields.

MS 406 serial no 269 used for training Polish pilots at Lyon-Bron.
SHAA

Fighters of the Polish Air Force

Polish instructors and cadets during training at Lyon-Bron in the spring of 1940.

SHAA

Polish fitter Stawidło. Photo was taken at Lyon-Mions.

K. Chołoniewski

Fighters ... **109**

Pilots of DAT Flight at Bourges. With commander of the Flight kpt. Kosinski.
Giermer coll.

Right:
Plut. Flanek of GC III/2. He was killed on 16 May 1940.
Lansoy via Persyn

Below:
Group photo of GC I/145 pilots. Photo was taken in May 1940, Lyon-Bron.
PI&SM.

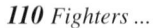

110 Fighters ...

Czech Fighters in France 1940
by Jiri Rajlich

After the collapse of Czechoslovakia in March 1939 many soldiers of the disbanded Czechoslovak army left their oppressed country. They intended to join one of the armies of the countries assumed to go to war with Germany soon. A lot of these emigrants were airmen.

By August 1939, almost 700 pilots and members of the ground-staff escaped to neighbouring Poland; but for most of them this was only a short stop on their way to France. However, the French representatives in Poland informed them that foreigners could not be enlisted in the French regular army in time of peace. The only solution was to sign a contract for five years military service in the Foreign Legion, which most of the Czechoslovak airmen, having no other possibility at the time, resolved to do. They took some comfort in the unwritten promise made by the French that, after the breakout of war, Czechoslovak soldiers would be enrolled in the French regular army. Between May and August 1939, 490 Czechoslovak airmen reached France by means of naval convoys from the Polish port of Gdynia. Another 20 arrived in France after a short stay in Great Britain. As there were still a lot of Czechoslovak soldiers making their way through the Balkans or released from Soviet prison camps, the number of Czechoslovak airmen coming to France increased gradually. In January 1940 as many as 584 soldiers of the Czechoslovak air force were in France; in March

An obsolete fighter plane, NiD.622 C.1 at Alzir-Maison Blanche air base. It bears the signs of 6. Escadrille GC III/4 in which a couple of Czechoslovak fighter pilots served. Some of them can be seen in this photograph.

J. Rajlich coll.

Czechoslovak pilots being trained on Morane-Saulnier MS.406C.1 fighter planes in Oran-La Senia. From left: por. Frantisek Bieberle (KIA 25 May 1940), por. Frantisek Vancl, Jici Kucera, rt. Vaclav Jicha (KIA 1 May 1945) and por. Vlastimil Vesely. The plane No 33 (N3 44) at that time belonged to the training unit GC I/9 but it was already provided with the insignia of its future user, 2. escadrille GC I/6, which after the training course was also joined by some of the pilots trained on this plane.

J. Rajlich coll.

1940 this number increased to 604 and in May to 786. As a result, the establishment of bigger units of the Czechoslovak air force became possible (despite problems in various areas).

When France entered the war, the French authorities kept their promise and the Czechoslovak airmen were transferred to airbases situated in the largest cities of France and in its North African territories. The unpleasant prospect of spending five years in the Foreign Legion was finally eliminated by the so-called "Czechoslovak" statute of 24 January 1940 which officially recognized the Czechoslovak soldiers as the members of the Czechoslovak army revived on French territory under the Franco-Czech agreement of 2 October 1939. Consequently, the Czechoslovak airmen legally ceased to be French soldiers and became servicemen of the Czechoslovak army with their original Czech ranks. They were to serve in the French units until the moment of establishing the Czech air forces. The 3rd Air Force Department of the Czechoslovak Military Command became the commanding organ of the Czechoslovak air force in France. It was led successively by pluk. Josef Berounsky, brig. gen. Karel Janousek (from December 1939), and brig. gen. Alois Vicherek (from March 1940).

The main task of the 3rd Air Force Department was to implement the agreement signed on 17 November 1939 which stipulated the creation of Czechoslovak air force units. Plans were made to form one fighter brigade which would include two fighter groups composed of two wings and eight squadrons. Subsequently, two bomber wings composed of four squadrons and an air force training centre were to be created. However, owing to the reluctance of the French authorities as well as to shortage of staff, an independent Czechoslovak air force unit failed to come into existence. The airmen, who from the beginning of December had been, in groups of three, drafted into the Armée de l'Air, did not form a separate unit.

The above-mentioned agreement designated Cognac, where during the First World War a Czechoslovak legion was formed, as the seat of a training and reserves corps of the Czechoslovak air forces. As in April 1940 the airbase in Cognac had not yet been completed, the training centre was temporarily located in the airport of Bordeaux-Merignac and also partly in Agde, where a reserves corps of the Czechoslovak army was based together with an airforce group. The Czechoslovak airmen, instructed mainly in employing French technology, were nevertheless trained not in Cognac but in over twenty training centres scattered all over France and in the French colonies.

The largest group of fighter pilots and ground-staff was trained at Chartres. Although it was a large base, airmen were trained also at Boulard and Bessay airbases. Moreover, to practice shooting pilots had to fly to the distant Caen-Carpiquet and Montpelier-Frejorques. The airmen trained at Chartres formed the core of Czechoslovak soldiers enrolled in the French air force. They were particularly successful in battles under French skies.

Other Czechoslovak airmen (mainly bomber pilots, observers, telegraphers and gunners) were trained at the airbases of Tours, Pau, Istres, Chateauroux, Tarbes and Toulouse-Francazacal. Smaller groups of airmen were trained also at the following centres: St. Jean d'Angeli (radio operators), Bourges (pilots' school), Le Bourget d'Etampes or La Rochelle (fighter pilots) as well as Cazaux (gunners).

The Czechoslovak airmen were also training in North Africa, mainly at the bases of Bilda, Oran-La Senia (fighter pilots) and Tafaraoui (bomber pilots).

The commander of the III. Air Force Department of CSVS, i.e. the commander of Czechoslovak air forces in France, gen. brig. Karel Janousek and st. kpt. Jaroslav Maly at the airbase where Czechoslovak airmen were trained. To the left rt. Josef Kubak, in the background Marcel Bloch MB.200 and MB.210 bombers.

Czechoslovak fighter pilots from ERC 571 (at the time 6. esc. GC III/4) and their French superiors. From left: rt. Karel Cap, rt. Josef Prihoda, S/Cf Lamonerie, Lt Avon, Cne Davy, S/Cf Girard, prap. Ondrej Posluzny, rt. Ladislav Zadrobilek and des. Frantisek Vindis. In the background, Dewoitine D.510C fighters. Algier-Maison, Blanche airbase, 20 January 1940.
Both photos J. Rajlich coll.

Fighters ... 113

Above:
A large proportion of the Czechoslovak fighter pilots at Chartres were trained on the American fighter plane, the Curtiss Hawk H-75C.1 (in the picture, plane No 55).

Both photos J. Rajlich coll.

Fighter pilots constituted the largest group of airmen who participated in front-line operations. They were sent to the Western Front from December. As already mentioned, they did not serve in separate Czechoslovak air force units but were in French squadrons. Until the end of the campaign in France, a total of 135 pilots were sent to operational fighter units of the Armée de l'Air. 113 of them fought against the Luftwaffe and the remaining 22 were assigned to defend the French colonies from the Italian Regia Aeronautica.

The list below is intended to provide the reader with at least some basic information on the units of the French Air Force in which Czechoslovak airmen served.

Curtiss H-75C.1 (version A-1) No 17 (X8 16), "blue 6" at Chartres airbase. It was piloted by des. Vladimír Vašek (KIA 2 January 1940), rt. F. Chábera and rt. O. Hanzlíeek (KIFA 10 October 1940), amongst others. The white tactical number 6 was also painted on the upper surface of the wing.

114 Fighters ...

Fighters of the Czechoslovak Air Force

Heinkel He111 W.Nr. 3327 (A1+CB) from I./KG 53, shot down by the pilots of GC II/5 in the first days of the German offensive.
J. Rajlich coll.

Czechoslovak fighter pilots in combat units of Armée de l´ Air 1939-1940

Unit	Number of Czech fighters*	Claims of Czech fighters — confirmed	Claims of Czech fighters — probables	Czech losses — KIA & MIA	Czech losses — WIA	Aircraft
GC I/1	6	1 1/2	1/2	2	2	MB-151, MB-152
GC III/1	3	1/7	-	-	-	MS-406
GC II/2	9	3 1/3	2/3	-	2	MS-406
GC I/3	3	1 2/3	1	1	1	D-520
GC II/3	6	10 1/4	-	2	3	MS-406, D-520
GC III/3	12	14 1/3	2 1/2	2	1	MS-406, D-520
GC I/4	5	1 1/3	-	-	2	H-75
GC II/4	4	4 1/6	-	-	1	H-75
GC III/4	5	-	-	-	-	NiD-622, D-510
GC I/5	9	13 1/3	1 1/3	3	3	H-75
GC II/5	8	9 1/4	3 1/2	-	2	H-75
GC III/5	2	-	-	-	-	NiD-622, D-510
GC I/6	19	12 1/3	1 1/2	4	4	MS-406
GC I/7	7	-	-	-	-	MS-406
GC III/7	9	-	-	2	1	MS-406
GC I/8	13	7 3/4	-	3	3	MB-151, MB-152
GC I/9	5	-	1	-	-	NiD-622, D-510, MS-406

*Some airmen served successively in several units

Fighters ... 115

Unit	Number of Czech fighters*	Claims of Czech fighters		Czech losses		aircraft
GC III/9	3	-	-	-	-	MB-151, MB-152
GC I/10	3	-	-	-	-	BS-510, MS-406
GC II/10	3	-	-	-	-	MB-152
GC III/10	3	-	-	-	-	MB-152
GC I/145	1	-	-	-	1	MS-406, C-714, MB-152
GR 4/108	1	-	-	-	-	MS-406
ELD Chartres	16	1	-	-	2	MS-406, MB-151
ELD Chateaudun	3	-	-	-	1	MS-406, MB-151
ELD I/55	3	-	-	-	1	MS-406, MB-151, VG 33
ERC 571	5	-	-	-	-	NiD-622, NiD-629, BS-510
ERC 572	1	-	-	-	-	NiD-622, BS-510
ERC 574	1	-	-	-	-	NiD-622, BS-510
Total		78 3/4	14 1/10	19	30	

*Some airmen served successively in several units

Czechoslovak pilots from GC II/2 learning from the map about the deteriorating war situation. From left: ppor. Bohumír Fürst, npor. Josef Hýbler, prap. Karel Šeda, prap. Stanislav Plzák and rt. František Bernard.
J. Rajlich coll.

Undoubtedly, the largest number of fighter pilots served in GC 1/6. They even formed the only Czechoslovak air force unit - the 1st Czechoslovak Fighter Squadron commanded by kpt. Jaroslav Kulhanek - which was brought into existence on 5 June 1940 (it was made retroactive to 18 May 1940). However, the events to come made its existence only an ephemeral phenomenon. Incomplete data, professional estimates and proportional calculations show that during the 'Phoney War' and in the Battle of France, Czechoslovak fighter pilots clocked up some 3800 flying hours in approximately 3000 operational flights (the largest number of flying hours was clocked up by the following pilots of GC III/3: rt. Vaclav Slouf - 91.30 hours, st. kpt. Evzen Cizek - 85.35 and prap. Josef Keprt - 78.30 hours). The above-mentioned numbers are almost certainly an underestimate.

Czechoslovak fighter pilots shot down or contributed to the shooting down of 129 enemy aircraft in total (algebraically adding the kills scored by Czechs alone and those scored in cooperation with the French we get the number 78.75 kills). The total number of probable kills scored by Czechs and those to which they probably contributed was 25 (algebraically adding 14.1). Losses inflicted by Czechoslovak fighter pilots in air raids against ground targets have never been calculated and most probably they will never be. Czechoslovak airmen paid a high price for their service in operational units: 18 of them were killed and 31 suffered injuries. The most spectacular successes were achieved by units equipped with Curtisses (Hawk 75s). In this group, GC I/5 with a high proportion of Czech airmen was particularly successful. It was in this unit that kpt. Alois Vasatko and por. Frantisek Perina - the two most successful Czechoslovak fighter pilots in the Battle of France - served. These two pilots were placed in the 5th and 9th positions, respectively, on the list of the most successful pilots of the Armée del'Air.

Remains of Marcel Bloch MB.151C.1 No 34 (Y5 21) "white 3", in which prap. Miloslav Rajtr was killed on 11 January 1940 during a training flight near Chartres.
J. Rajlich coll.

Jiri Rajlich

Above:
The first Czechoslovak airman shot down in an air fight in the West, des. Karel Körber from GC II/3. He was hit fighting Hptm. Werner Mölders in the area of Toul-Croix-de-Metz. Although he was wounded he managed to land in his MS.406C.1.

Above right: Marcel Bloch MB.151C.1 No 352 at the training airbase at Chartres. In front of the plane you can see one of the Czechoslovak pilots st. kpt. Jaroslav Malý, a pre-war Czechoslovak air attache in Berlin. The figure of Donald Duck with a club was the insignia of one of the training escadrilles CIC No 6 at Chartres.

Right: A valuable picture taken from a MS.406C.1 from Chartres training airbase
during one of the training flights near the base. In the cockpit you can see
one of the Czechoslovak pilots.

All Photos J. Rajlich coll.

118 Fighters ...

Fighters of the Czechoslovak Air Force

Left:
Pilots of II./JG 53 Ace of Spades, who routed a group of MS.406C.1s from GC III/7 over Morhange on 31 March 1940. From left: Hptm. Günther von Maltzahn, Oblt. Heinz Bretnütz, Uffz. Werner Kaufmann, Lt. Schröder and Fw. Albrecht Baun. One of the Moranes they shot down was piloted by a Czech airman, por. Bedoich Dvooák who, despite a wounded leg, managed to crash-land at Vitry-le-Francois airbase.
M. Souffan

Opposite page, centre:
Chartres, December 1939. The first group of Czechoslovak officers leaves for the front. From left: npor. Timotheus Hamsik (GC I/5, KIA 14 May 1940), npor. Antonin Mikolasek (GC II/3, KIA 25 May 1940), kpt. Jindrich Beran (GC III/3, KIA 12 May 1940), st. kpt. Eížek (GC III/3, KIFA 26 November 1942), npor. Antonín Navrátil (GC I/8), npor. Jioí Král (GC I/1, KIA 8 June 1940), npor. Josef Jaške (GC II/5) and npor. Jan Klán (GC II/5).
J. Rajlich coll.

Left:
The Duke of Windsor, formerly King Edward VIII, inspecting a new Dewoitine D.520C.1 at Cannes-Mandelieu airbase in the spring of 1940.
J. Rajlich coll.

Fighters ... 119

Jiri Rajlich

Above:
On 23 April 1940 while pursuing a reconnaissance Do17Z of 1.(H)/13 this Curtiss H-75C.1 No 198 from GC II/5 was shot by a German plane. The pilot, npor. Josef Jaške (in the picture he is inside), managed to crash-land at Pont á Mousson.

Right:
A number of French planes were destroyed during surprise air attacks against airbases. In the picture you can see the burnt remains of a Curtiss H-75 from GC II/4 at Xafféviller. This attack was carried out by six Messerschmitt Bf109s and one Bf110 on 12 May 1940 - the Germans set fire to 5 Curtisses and wounded five men from the ground staff. Surprised anti-aircraft staff did not fire a single shot, except for one of the guns whose shells hit one of the 109s.

Right:
A Curtiss H-75 from 3. escadrille GC II/5 flying over the front line.

All photos J. Rajlich coll.

120 Fighters ...

The top Czech fighter aces in the Battle of France

Rank and name	GC	Battle of France score *	Remarks
kpt. Alois Vašátko	I/5	3+9 confirmed, 0+2 probables	WIA 26. 5. 1940, KIA 23. 6. 1942
por. František Peřina	I/5	2+9 confirmed, 2 probables	WIA 3. 6. 1940
rt. Václav Cukr	II/3	3+5 confirmed	WIA 8. 6. 1940, WIFA 4. 7. 1943
npor. Tomáš Vybíral	I/5	1+6 confirmed	
rt. Josef Stehlík	III/3	2+4 confirmed, 0+1 probables	
rt. František Chábera	II/5	3+2 confirmed, 1+1 probables	
npor. Jan Klán	II/5	2+3 confirmed, 3 probables	
škpt. Evžen Čížek	III/3	2+3 confirmed	KIFA 26. 11. 1942
rt. Ladislav Světlík	II/5	0+4 confirmed, 0+3 probables	
rt. Václav Jícha	I/6	2+2 confirmed	KIFA 1. 2. 1945

(3+9 stands for 3 destroyed aircraft + 9 destroyed in co-operation)

A Curtiss H-75C.1 No 35 ("white 5") from 3. escadrille GC II/5. Although its German counterpart, the Messerschmitt Bf 109 E was faster, the Curtiss was one of the best planes the French had. Many Czechoslovaks were very successful flying Curtisses.

SHAA

Besides fighter pilots, bomber pilots also took part in operational flights. However, their achievements were of no great significance. At least 26 pilots, telegraphers and gunners fought in five combat and bomber units. According to incomplete data, they made 134 operational flights totalling 390 hours. They served in the following units:

However, it would be unfair to mention only the flying personnel, that is pilots, telegraphers or gunners who participated in the campaign in France. The "airmen without wings" - not very nobly labelled as ground-staff members - are very often ignored. This concerns primarily the mechanics and armourers. At least 44 of them served in operational units alongside their pilot colleagues. The bulk of them took care of the machines in extremely difficult conditions. Their performance, especially during the enemy air-

Unit – the number of Czechoslovak airmen – armament

Unit	No of Czech pilots	Aircraft
GB I/21	4	MB-210, Amiot 351/354
GB II/21	5	MB-210, Amiot A-351/354
GB I/23	3	MB-210, LeO-451
GBA II/35	3	Bré 691/693
GBA II/54	2	Bré 691/693, Potez 633

raids, deserves the deepest respect. On 21 May 1940, during an air-raid on the airport in Cormeiles-en-Vexin, one of the mechanics of GC III/3 - prap. Jan Prokop - shot down one Dornier Do 17.

In summary, we should note that Czechoslovak fighter pilots formed a substantial part of the frontline units of the French air force. They constituted 12 per cent of the entire fighter forces of the Armée de l'Air. In other words, every eighth fighter pilot in the French air forces was Czechoslovak. That is also the case with the successes achieved by Czechoslovak fighter pilots - 12% of the planes destroyed by the pilots of the French air force were shot down by Czechs.

Their successes resulted in signing (on 1 June 1940) a new agreement on the establishment of independent Czechoslovak fighter and bomber squadrons. It was, however, too late. Until the collapse of France no bigger Czechoslovak air force unit was brought into existence. This resulted both from the reluctance of the French authorities as well as from shortage of staff. First of all, however, it was the consequence of the fact that on 17 June 1940 France asked for peace and the capitulation act was signed five days later. Czechoslovak airmen had died in vain.

Fighters of the Czechoslovak Air Force

Pilots from GC II/5 by one of their victims, a Heinkel He111 bomber from KG 55, shot down in the first days of the German offensive. To the left, in the middle (with no cap) npor. Jan Klán (5+3 kills), to the right the commander of the group Cdt. Marcel Hugues.
J. Rajlich coll.

After the capitulation of France, Czechoslovak soldiers were making their way to Great Britain by whatever means they could - mainly by means of naval convoys. By August 1940 as many as 932 airmen (97% of the last noted number of Czechoslovak airmen in France) reached the British coast.

Kpt. Alois Vašátko.

(25 August 1908, Celakovice k/Prahy - 23 June 1942, Kanal, to the east of Start Point)

He was the most successful Czechoslovak fighter pilot and one of the outstanding officers of the Czechoslovak air force during the Second World War. In 1927 he graduated from the Pedagogical Institute in Hradec Kralove and then worked as a teacher in Litomerice. Thanks to his pedagogical inclinations he was later nicknamed Amos. In 1928, he joined the army and as an artillery man began what was to become a brilliant career as a fighter pilot. As a regular soldier he served in the 3. and 52. Artillery Regiment in Litomerice and Josefov. Later, he decided to become a professional soldier and studied at the Military Academy in Hranice, from which he graduated with the rank of artillery lieutenant. Subsequently, he served in the 54. and 7. Artillery Regiments in Bratislava and Olomouc, where he was promoted to the rank of nadporucik. In 1935 he was sent to a course for lookouts at LVU in Prostejov. As an observer he served in the 2. Air Force Squadron at Olomouc. At the end of 1936 he moved from artillery to air forces. In 1937-38 he completed a training course for pilots and took command of the 14. Reconnaissance Wing equipped with Letov S-328 biplanes. He served in this unit till the beginning of the German occupation.

In June 1939 he left Czechoslovakia and reached France through Poland. After the outbreak of the Second World War, he completed training courses

Kpt. Alois Vašátko.
J. Rajlich coll.

Fighters ... *123*

Two of the Czechoslovak members of GC II/5 - pilot prap. František Chábera (5+2 kills) and mechanic prap. Vilém Nosek. Behind them Curtiss H-75C.1 No 58 ("white 1"), with the painting of the head of a Sioux Indian – the insignia of the planes from 3. escadrille GC II/5.

All photos J. Rajlich coll.

on fighter planes in Chartres. In 1940, he was sent to the front and joined the famous GC I/5 equipped with Curtiss Hawk H-75 fighters. GC I/5 was the most successful unit in the French air forces, in which a lot of Czech airmen served. Some of them, for example Frantisek Perina and Tomas Vybiral, earned the status of ace pilots. During the five hectic weeks on the French front Alois Vasatko clocked up a total of 52 operational hours. He achieved 12 certain and 2 probable victories. With this record he became the most successful Czechoslovak fighter pilot partcipating in the campaign in France. It also placed him in 5th position on the list of the fighter aces of the French air forces. He was injured on 26 May 1940 in an engagement with the enemy.

A pilot from GC II/5, prap. Otto Hanzlíeek (2+1 kills). On 18 May 1940 near Metz Hanzlíeek was shot down by Lt. Günther Rall from 8./JG 52. It was the first of the 275 kills he scored altogether. Hanzlíeek survived using his parachute.

After the defeat of France he flew with his unit to North Africa and, subsequently, he reached Great Britain making his way through the Straits of Gibraltar on a boat. He was commissioned in the RAF with the rank of Pilot Officer and in September 1940 he became one of the founders of the 312 (Czechoslovak) Fighter Squadron. In this unit he flew, successively, Hurricane Mk./I/ IIA/IIB and Spitfire Mk. IIA/IIB/VB. He participated in the Battle of Britain and in operations over occupied France as part of the Kenley Wing. At the same time he was constantly increasing the number of his victories. In November 1940 he took on the command of B Flight, and in June 1941 he became the commander of 312 Squadron. He was also the first commander of the so-called Exeter Czechoslovak Wing. He was killed on 23 June 1942, while leading his wing back to England, accompanied by Bostons which had dropped their bombs on the airport in Morlaix. Near the British coast his Spitfire ran into a Fw190 piloted by Wilhelm Reuschling from III/JG Richthofen. Vasatko's plane fell into the sea. His body has never been found.

During two years on the Western Front Alois Vasatko was credited with destroying 14 enemy aircraft (plus 4 probably and 1 damaged). He died in the rank of stabni kapitan, he was in memoriam promoted to podplukovnik and in 1992 to the rank of general major.

For his unusual combat effectiveness he was awarded three times the Czechoslovak Military Cross, two times with the Medal of Courage, Memorial Medal of the Army Abroad (F-VB), three times the MRS Medal, the French Croix de Guerre with seven palms, two Silver and one Golden Star, the medal of the order of Legion d'Honneur (in the rank of Chevalier), the British Distinguished Flying Cross, the 1939-1945 Star (with Battle of Britain Clasp), Air Crew Europe Star, Defence Medal and War Medal.

Prap. František Chábera (5+2 kills) by his Curtiss, which bears the insignia of his unit, 4. Escadrille GC II/5.

J. Rajlich coll.

Jiri Rajlich

Above:
Curtiss Hawk H-75C.1 No 140 (U0 70) "white 11" in the colours of 3. escadrille GC II/5, the unit in which prap. Otto Hanzlíeek, st. kpt. Josef Duda and prap. František Chábera, amongst others, served. The plane was initially used for training Czechoslovak pilots at Chartres. At that time it bore the tactical number "black 1". Although the number was changed from 1 to 11 the plane still had a white 1 on the upper surface of the wing.

Middle of the page:
A Czechoslovak pilot from GC II/4, prap. Karel Pošta, posing for a photograph by a captured Messerschmitt Bf109E (W. Nr. 3247, 54 Grünherz. On 30 May 1940 a German pilot, Uffz. Karl Hager, mistakenly landed on the French side. His plane

Another Czechoslovak pilot from GC II/4, prap. Jan Truhlář posing by the same plane.

126 Fighters ...

was secured by French and Czechoslovak airmen. It was immediately provided with French markings and sent to the rear.
Another Czechoslovak pilot from GC II/4, prap. Jan Truhláo posing by the same plane.

Top of this page:
Camouflaged fighter plane Dewoitine D.520C.1 No 129 from 2. escadrille GC I/3 waits for the alert. Three Czechoslovak pilots served in this unit, one of them died (npor. Otakar Korec).

Left:
Npor. Jan Eermák, one of the numerous Czechoslovak pilots in GC III/3, by his plane after the withdrawal to North Africa. Dewoitine D.520C.1s were the best fighter planes the Armée de l'Air could send against the Luftwaffe. However, very few of them came into service prior to the Armistice.

Bottom:
The fight with a Bf109 on 6 June 1940 ended for por. František Burda from GC I/4 in a crash-landing and an accident near Bernay. Curtiss H-75C.1 No 212 "black 3" was not seriously damaged. Burda shot down one Bf 109.
All photos J. Rajlich coll.

Fighters ... 127

Jiri Rajlich

Top:
Dewoitine D.520 C.1s from GC III/3 after the withdrawal to North Africa. Relizane airbase, the end of June 1940.

Middle:
Curtiss H-75C.1 No 63 (X8 62) "white 7" from 4. escadrille GC II/5 at St. Denis du Sig, June 1940. During the Battle of France this plane was flown by st. kpt. Josef Duda.

Right:
The evacuation of Czechoslovak airmen from North Africa to Great Britain. The most successful Czechoslovak fighter pilot of the Battle of France, kpt. Alois Vašátko, is playing cards.

All photos J. Rajlich coll.

128 Fighters ...

In Colour

Above: He 111s of 4./KG 27 during a bombing raid on Belgium. (TVB)

Below: A Curtiss Hawk H 75 A4, with Pratt & Whitney R-1830, captured by the Germans at Bourges. (TVB)

Fighters ... *129*

A close-up of the wreckage at Bourges.
(TVB)

Wrecked Curtis and Breguet at Bourges airfield.
(TVB)

A Curtiss H-75A-2, n° 126 also pictured by Dr. Barke of KG 27 at Bourges.
T. Kopański coll.

Above:
The destroyed Fiat CR 42 of 3./II./2. Aé. at Brustem airfield.
Below:
Crew of KG 27 inspect the burned Fiat at Brustem airfield.

Both photos P. Taghon coll.

Colour Wartime Photos

Close up photo of captured Curtis Hawk H 75 A4, at Bourges.
T. Kopański coll.

Bf 109 E-3 of III./JG51 in France 1940, just after Dunkirk. Aircraft belonged to the Technical Officer, Oblt. Werner Pichon-Kalau von Hofe
R. Pęczkowski coll.

132 Fighters ...

Colour Profiles

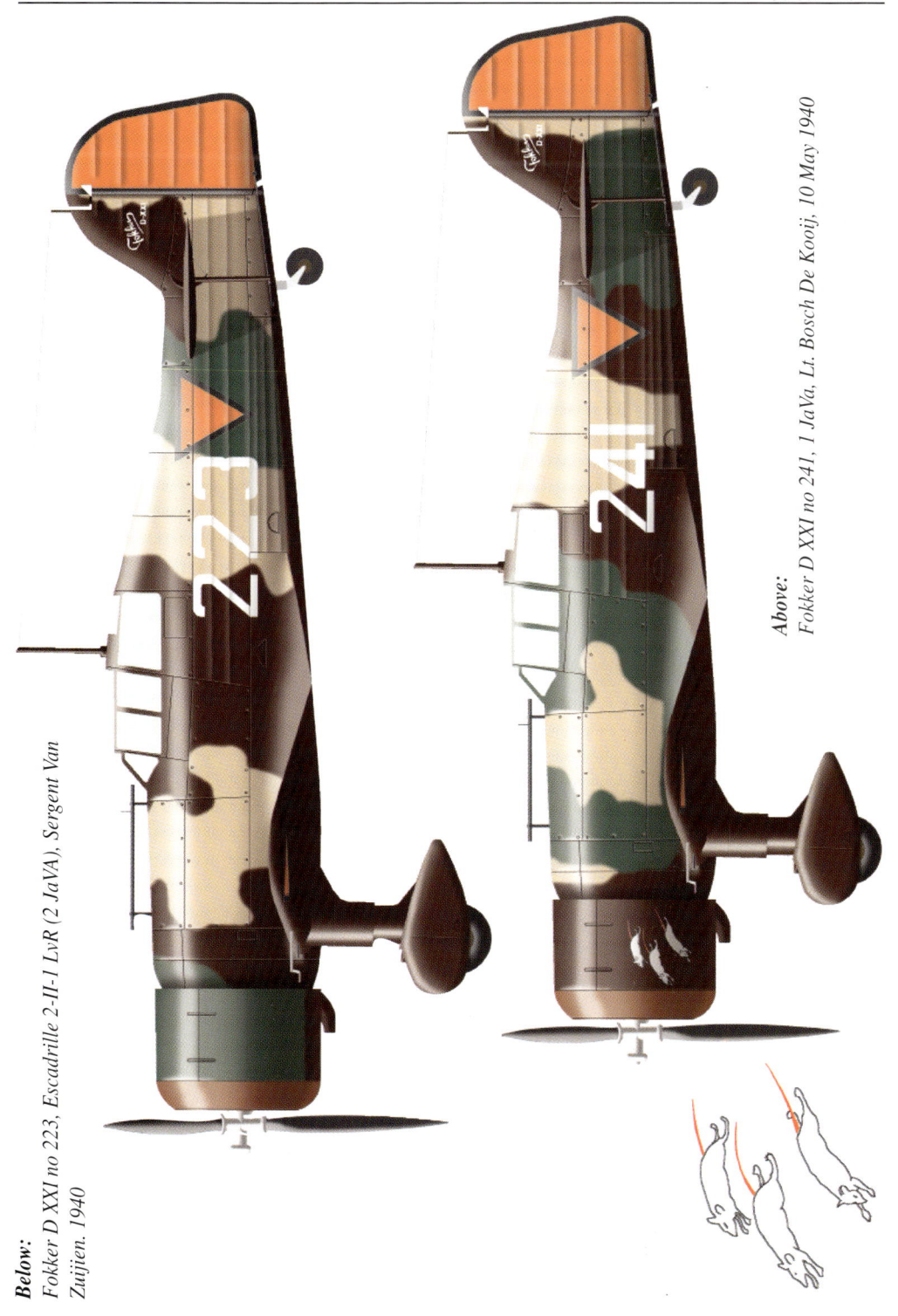

Above:
Fokker D XXI no 241, 1 JaVa, Lt. Bosch De Kooij, 10 May 1940

Below:
Fokker D XXI no 223, Escadrille 2-II-1 LvR (2 JaVA), Sergent Van Zuijien, 1940

Fighters ... 133

Artur Juszczak

134 Fighters ...

Colour Profiles

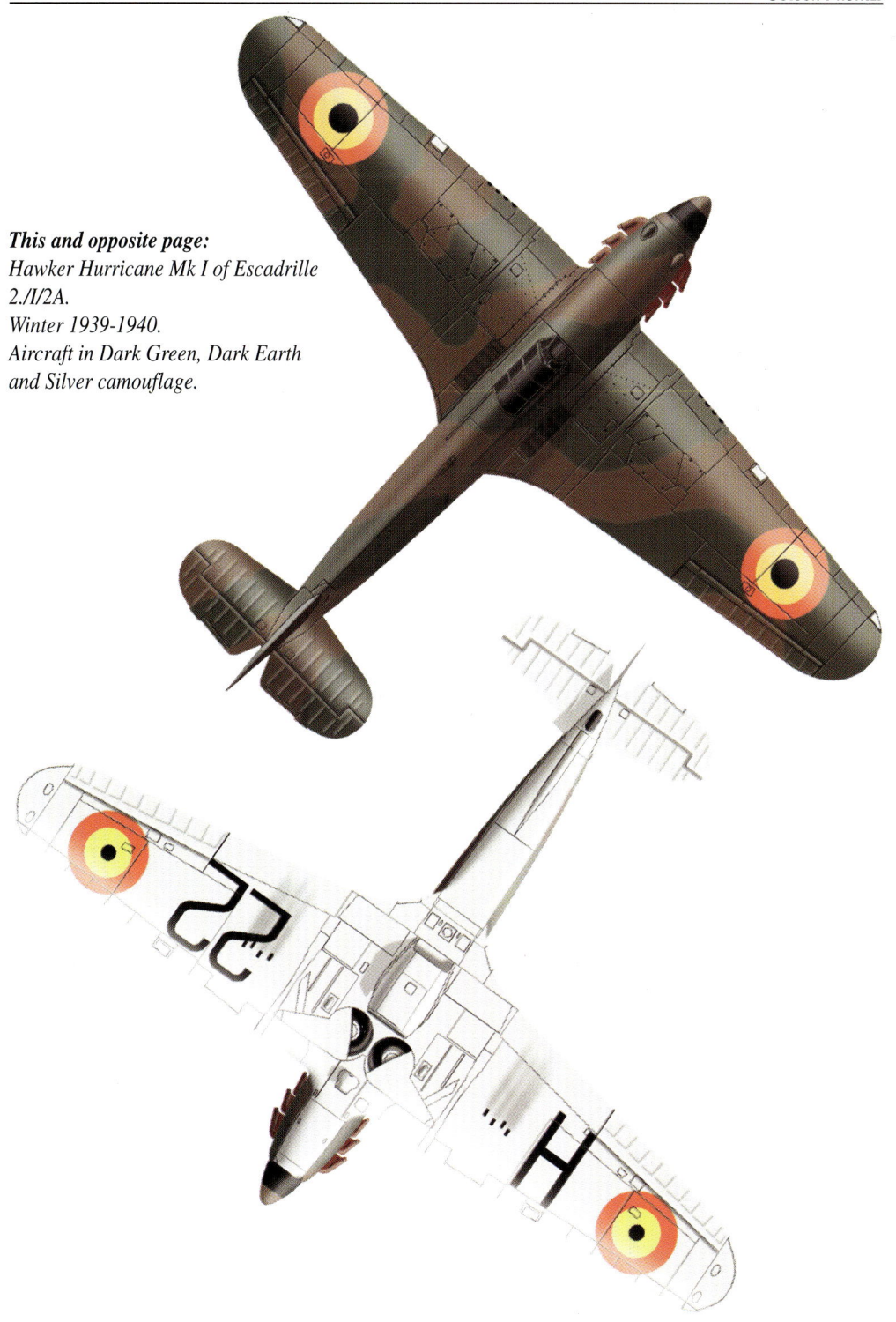

This and opposite page:
Hawker Hurricane Mk I of Escadrille 2./I/2A.
Winter 1939-1940.
Aircraft in Dark Green, Dark Earth and Silver camouflage.

Fighters ... **135**

Artur Juszczak

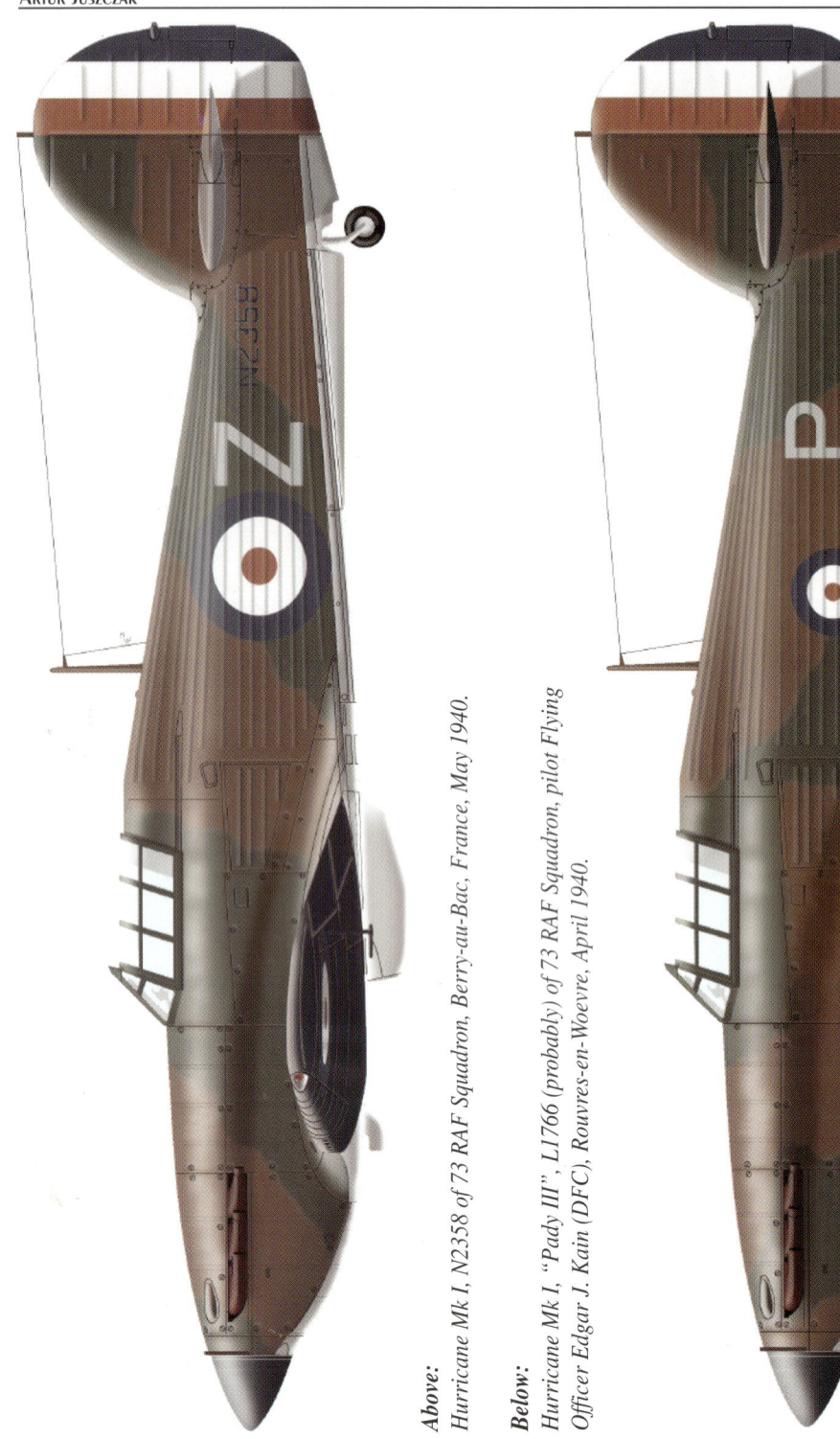

Above:
Hurricane Mk I, N2358 of 73 RAF Squadron, Berry-au-Bac, France, May 1940.

Below:
Hurricane Mk I, "Pady III", L1766 (probably) of 73 RAF Squadron, pilot Flying Officer Edgar J. Kain (DFC), Rouvres-en-Woevre, April 1940.

136 Fighters ...

Colour Profiles

Above:
Gloster Gladiator Mk I, "32" of 1 Escadrille, Belgian Royal Air Force, 1939. Khaki Green upper surfaces and aluminium dope under surfaces.
Below:
Gloster Gladiator Mk II, KW-T of 615 Squadron RAF, France 1940.

Below:
Gloster Gladiator Mk II, N2001, KW-R of 615 Squadron RAF(AASF), North France 1940.

Fighters ... 137

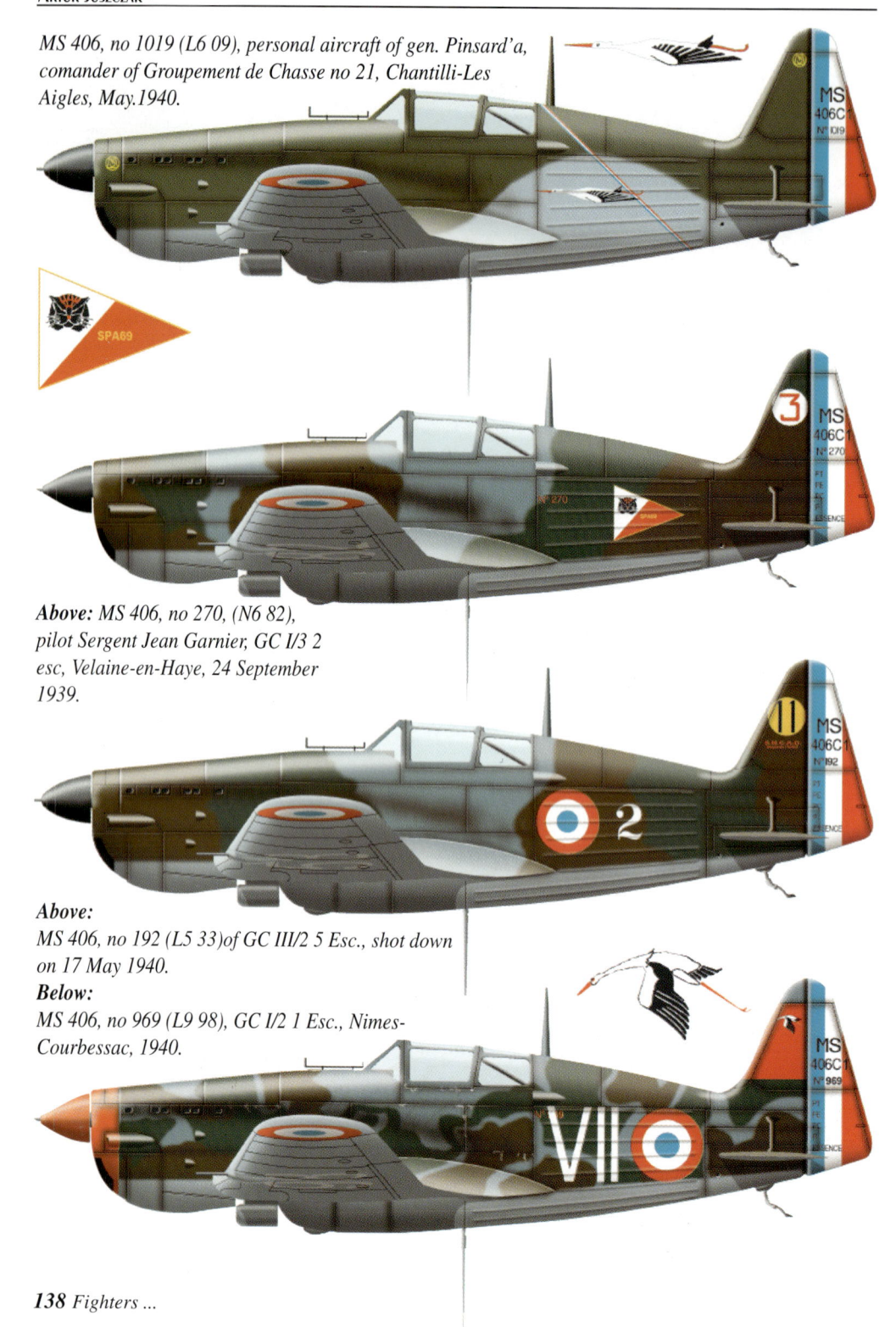

MS 406, no 1019 (L6 09), personal aircraft of gen. Pinsard'a, comander of Groupement de Chasse no 21, Chantilli-Les Aigles, May.1940.

Above: MS 406, no 270, (N6 82), pilot Sergent Jean Garnier, GC I/3 2 esc, Velaine-en-Haye, 24 September 1939.

Above:
MS 406, no 192 (L5 33) of GC III/2 5 Esc., shot down on 17 May 1940.
Below:
MS 406, no 969 (L9 98), GC I/2 1 Esc., Nimes-Courbessac, 1940.

138 Fighters ...

Colour Profiles

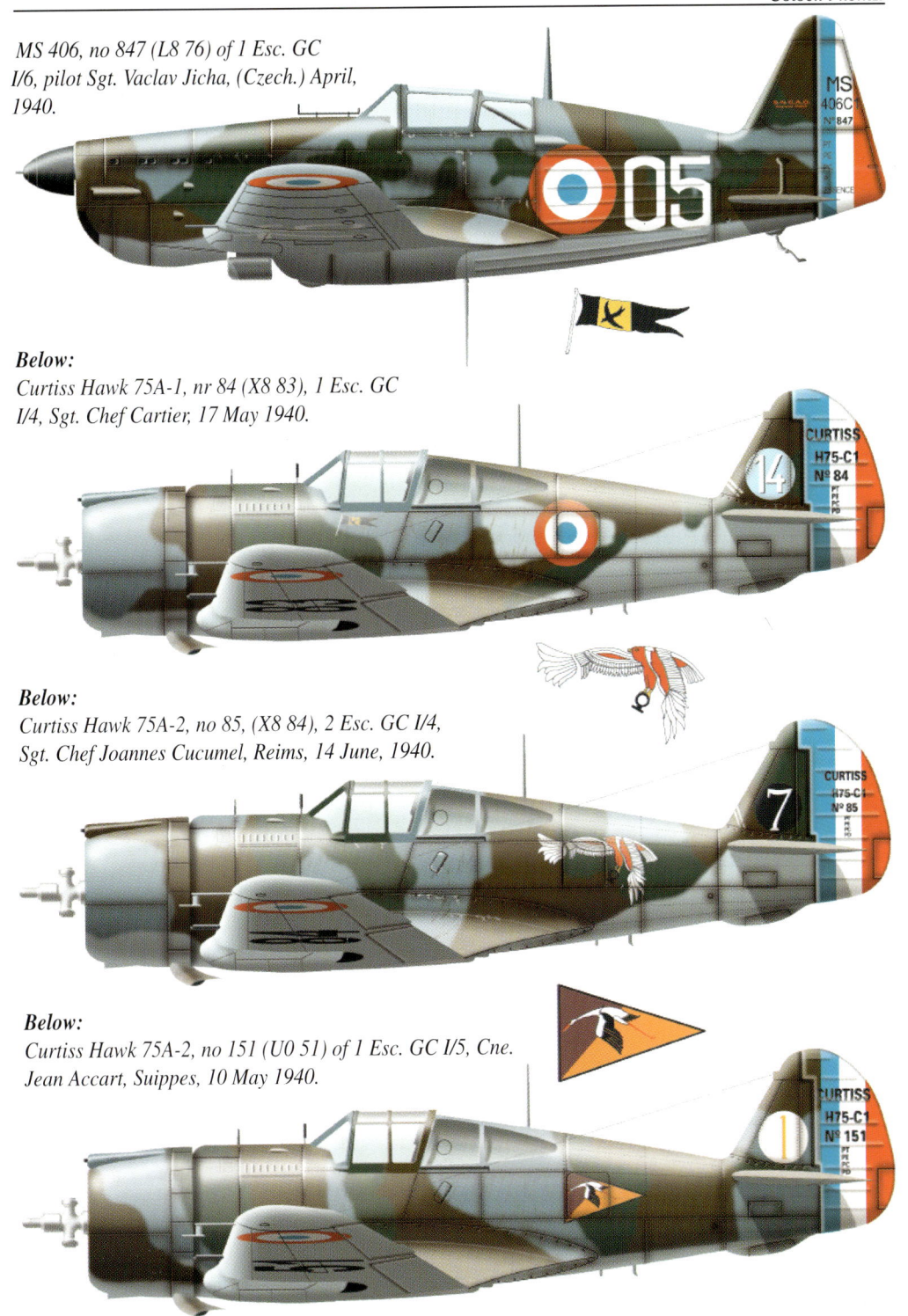

MS 406, no 847 (L8 76) of 1 Esc. GC I/6, pilot Sgt. Vaclav Jicha, (Czech.) April, 1940.

Below:
Curtiss Hawk 75A-1, nr 84 (X8 83), 1 Esc. GC I/4, Sgt. Chef Cartier, 17 May 1940.

Below:
Curtiss Hawk 75A-2, no 85, (X8 84), 2 Esc. GC I/4, Sgt. Chef Joannes Cucumel, Reims, 14 June, 1940.

Below:
Curtiss Hawk 75A-2, no 151 (U0 51) of 1 Esc. GC I/5, Cne. Jean Accart, Suippes, 10 May 1940.

Fighters ... **139**

Artur Juszczak

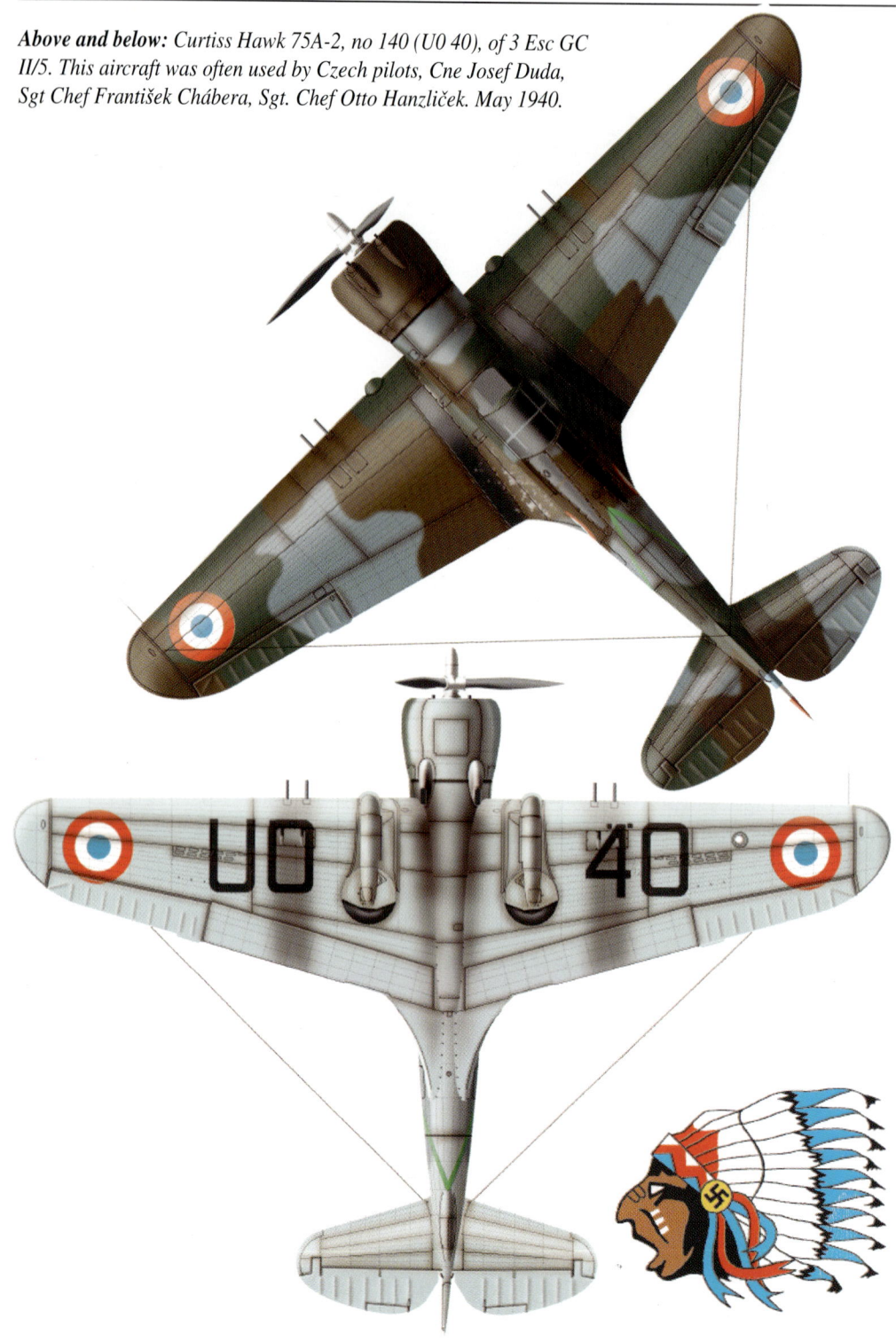

Above and below: *Curtiss Hawk 75A-2, no 140 (U0 40), of 3 Esc GC II/5. This aircraft was often used by Czech pilots, Cne Josef Duda, Sgt Chef František Chábera, Sgt. Chef Otto Hanzliček. May 1940.*

140 Fighters ...

Colour Profiles

Above and below: Curtiss Hawk 75A-2, no 140 (U0 40), of 3 Esc GC II/5.

Above: Curtiss Hawk 75A-2, no 279, Sgt. Chef Antoine Casenobe, 3 Esc. GC II/4, Marignane, 1940.

Above: Curtiss Hawk 75A-2, no 198 (U0 97), of 4 Esc, GC II/5. 23 May 1940 aircraft piloted by por. Josef Jaske (Czech), was shot down by German Flak.

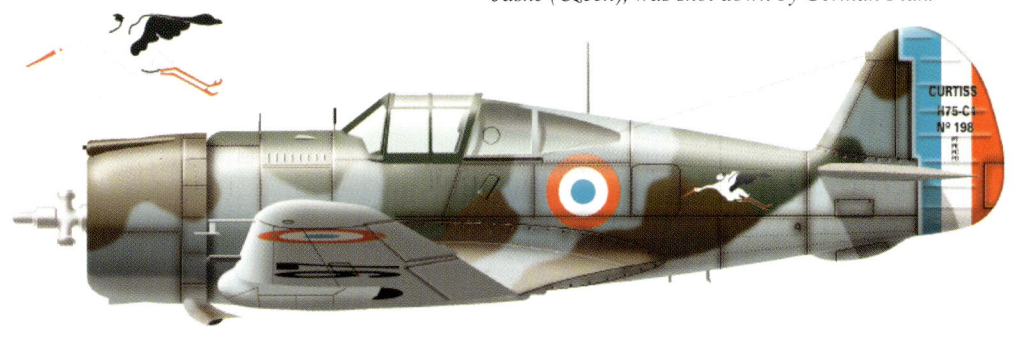

Fighters ... **141**

Artur Juszczak

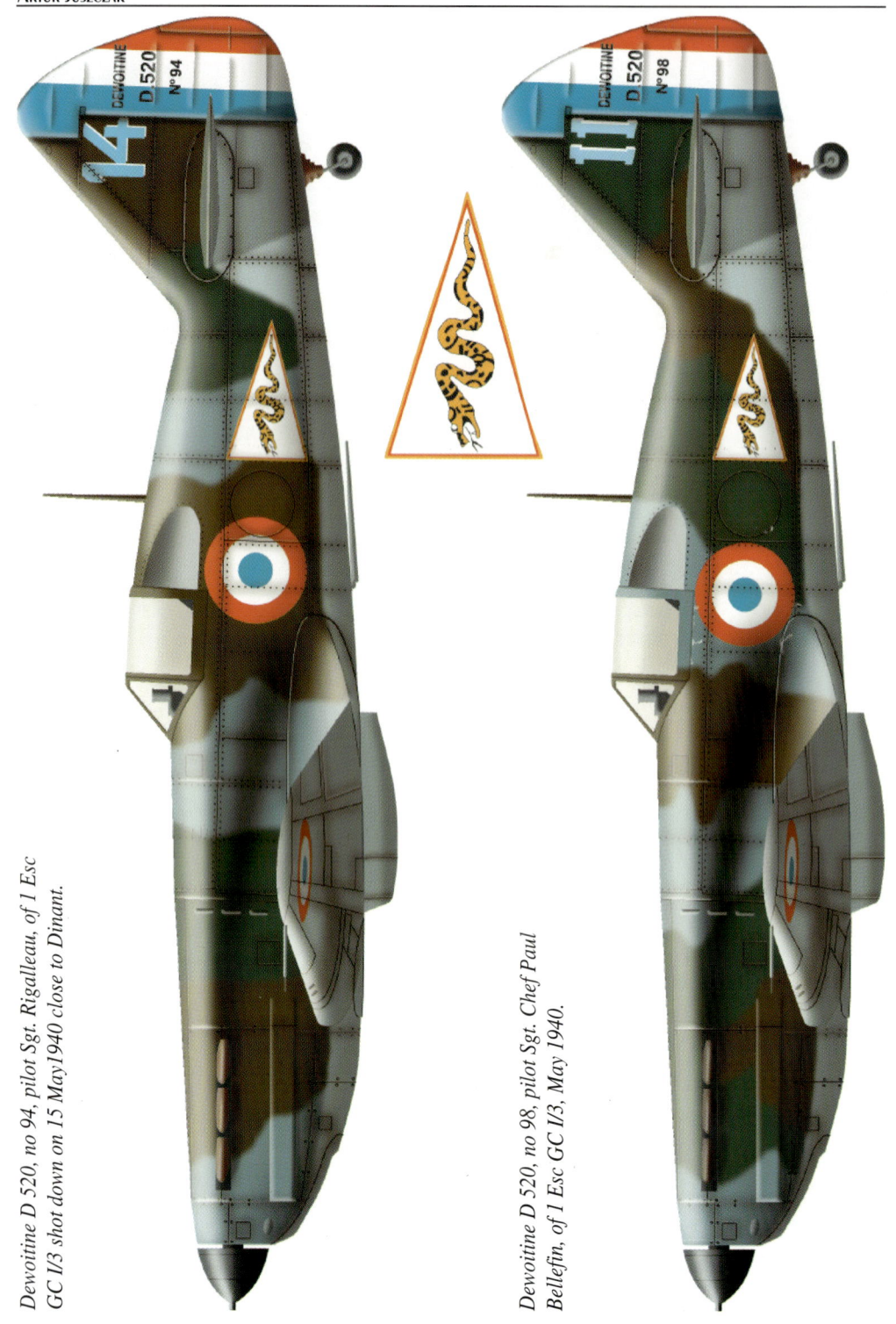

Dewoitine D 520, no 94, pilot Sgt. Rigalleau, of 1 Esc GC I/3 shot down on 15 May 1940 close to Dinant.

Dewoitine D 520, no 98, pilot Sgt. Chef Paul Bellefin, of 1 Esc GC I/3, May 1940.

142 Fighters ...

Colour Profiles

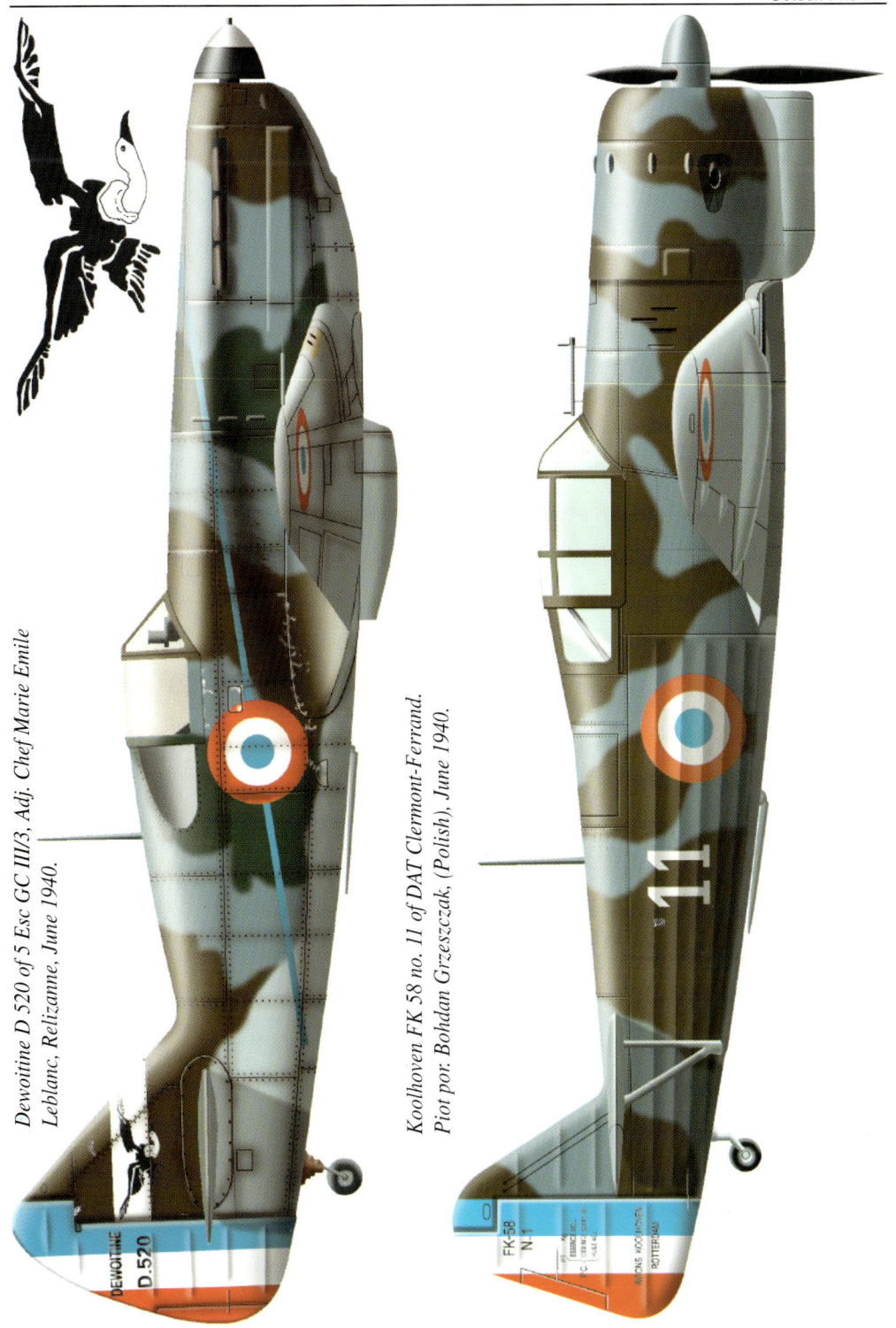

Dewoitine D 520 of 5 Esc GC III/3, Adj. Chef Marie Emile Leblanc, Relizanne, June 1940.

Koolhoven FK 58 no. 11 of DAT Clermont-Ferrand. Piot por. Bohdan Grzeszczak, (Polish), June 1940.

Fighters ... **143**

Artur Juszczak

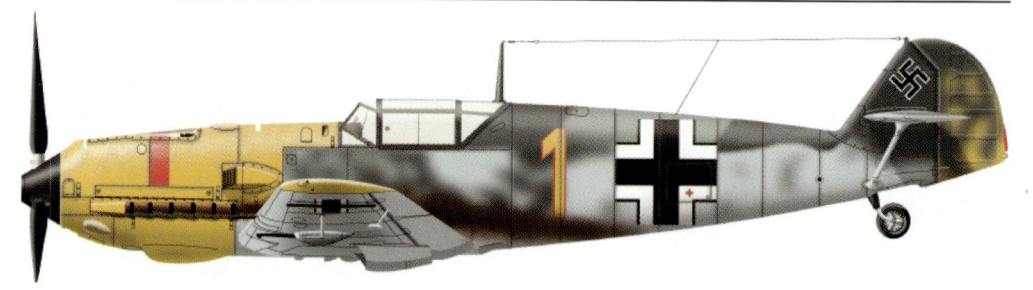

Above: Messerschmitt Bf 109E-3, probably 2./JG53, July 1940, France. Camouflage RLM 71/02/65 plus blotches of 70 on the fuselage sides.
Below: Messerschmitt Bf 109E-3, W.Nr 5102 of I/JG77, May 1940, Orendorf, France. Personal aircraft of Gruppen Adjutant. Camouflage RLM 71/02/65.

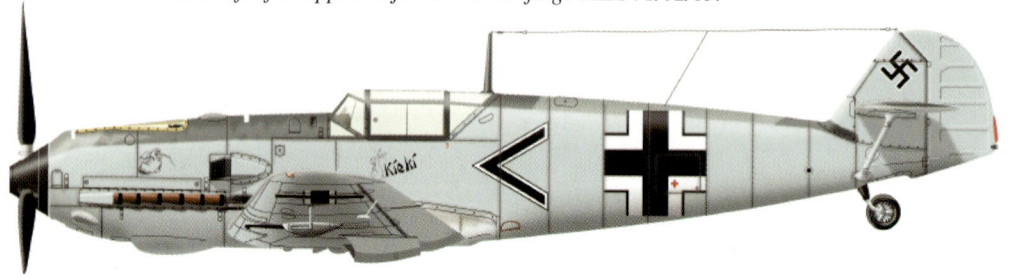

Below: Messerschmitt Bf 109 E-3 of 7./JG2, pilot Oberfeldfebel Werner Machold, Cambrai, 27 May 1940. Camouflage 71/02/65 with small patches in 71.

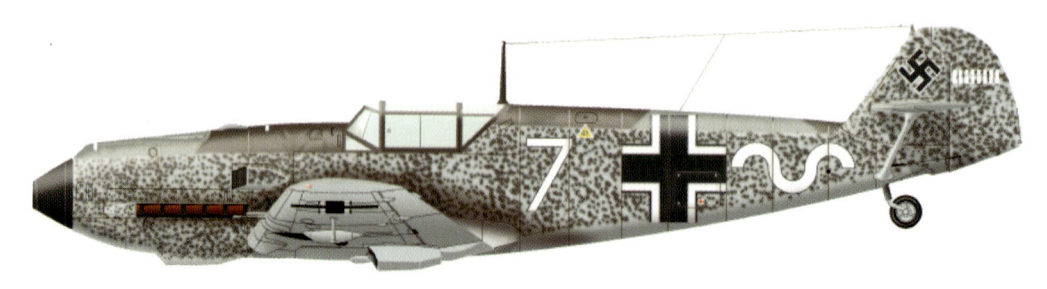

Below: Messerschmitt Bf 109 E-3 Gruppenkomandeur III./JG26 Adolf Galland, France, 1940. Camouflage 71/02/65.

144 Fighters ...

Colour Profiles

Above: Messerschmitt Bf 110C of 4./ZG 1, feldwebel Otto Beiter Obergefraiter Hink.
Below: Messerschmitt Bf 110C of 3./ZG 26 W.nr 3011, feldwebel H. Reimann, obergefraiter H. Röwe. Aircraft was shot down on 10 May 1940 by French pilot of GC I/5, sgt. Morel.

Fighters ... **145**

Artur Juszczak

This and opposite page:
Messerschmitt Bf 109 E-3 of Werner Mölders.
All upper surfaces are in RLM 02. Lower surfaces in RLM 65. Top of the fuselage and upper surfaces of the wings and horizontal stabiliser sprayed with RLM 70, as are the blotches on the rudder. Shapes of the blotches on the wings are in part estimated. On the fin are 18 kill bars marked in white. This camouflage was used only by JG 53 during Air War over France.

146 Fighters ...

Colour Profiles

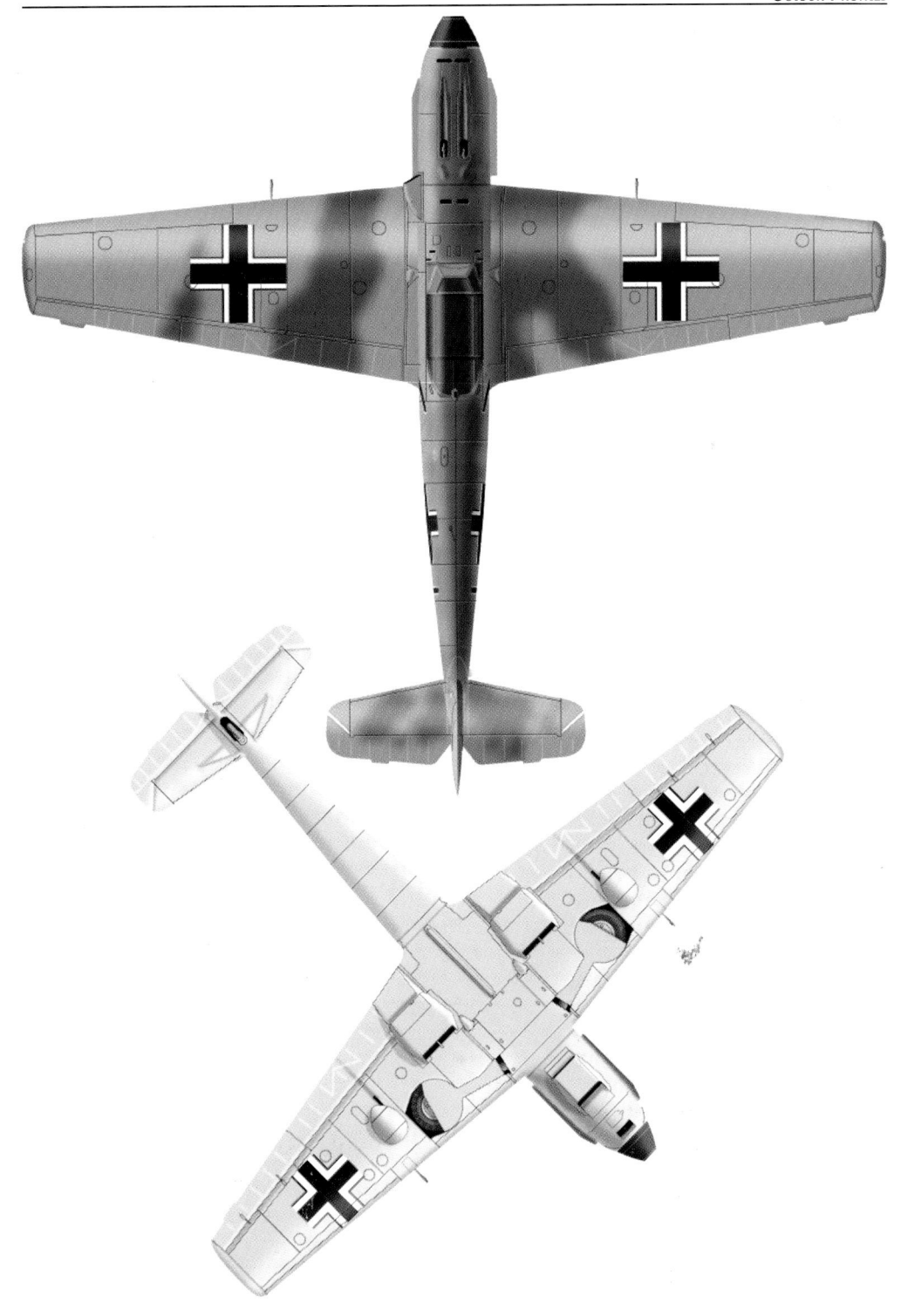

Fighters ... 147

Artur Juszczak

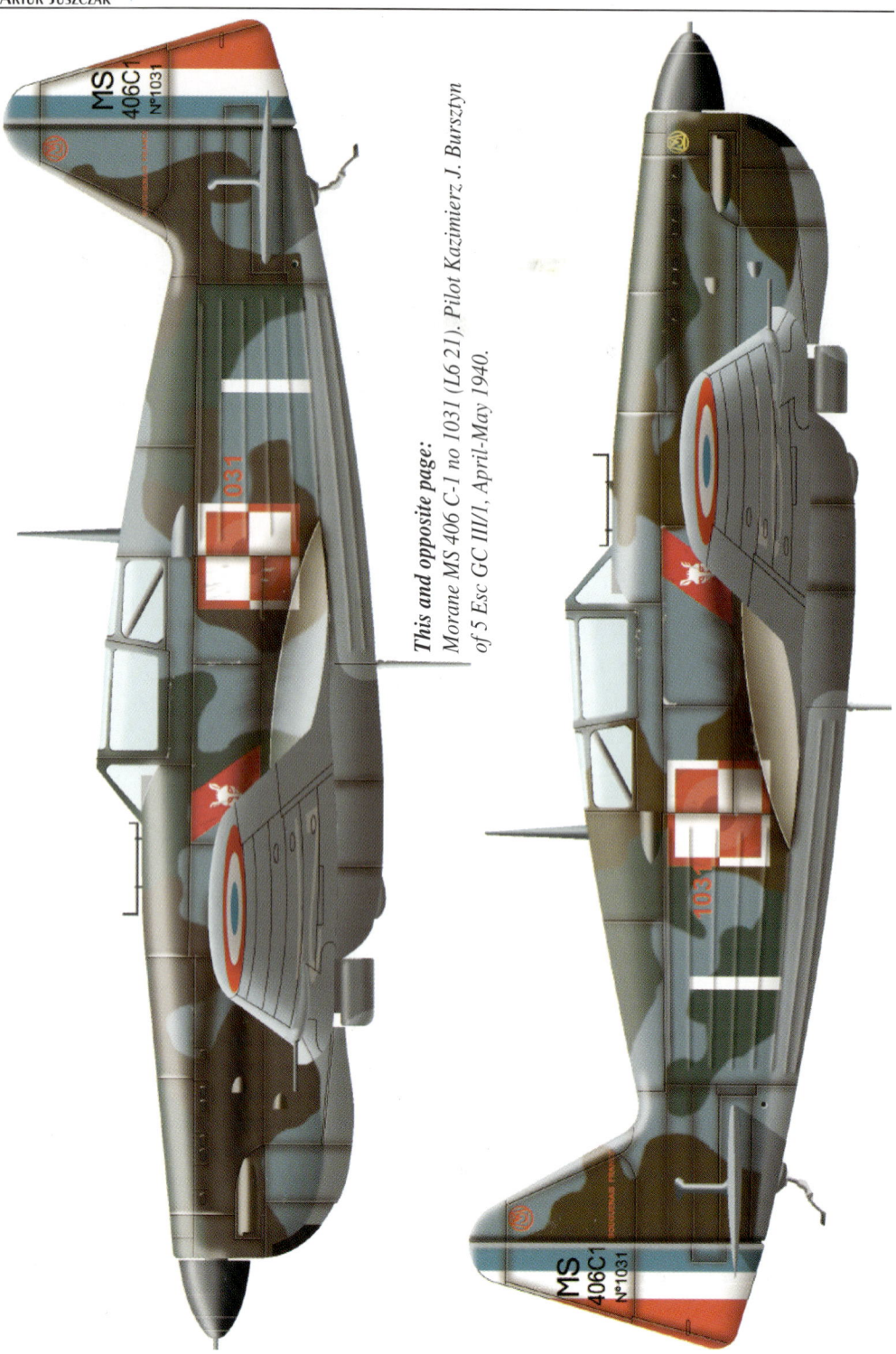

This and opposite page:
Morane MS 406 C-1 no 1031 (L6 21). Pilot Kazimierz J. Bursztyn of 5 Esc GC III/1, April-May 1940.

148 Fighters ...

Colour Profiles

Fighters ... 149

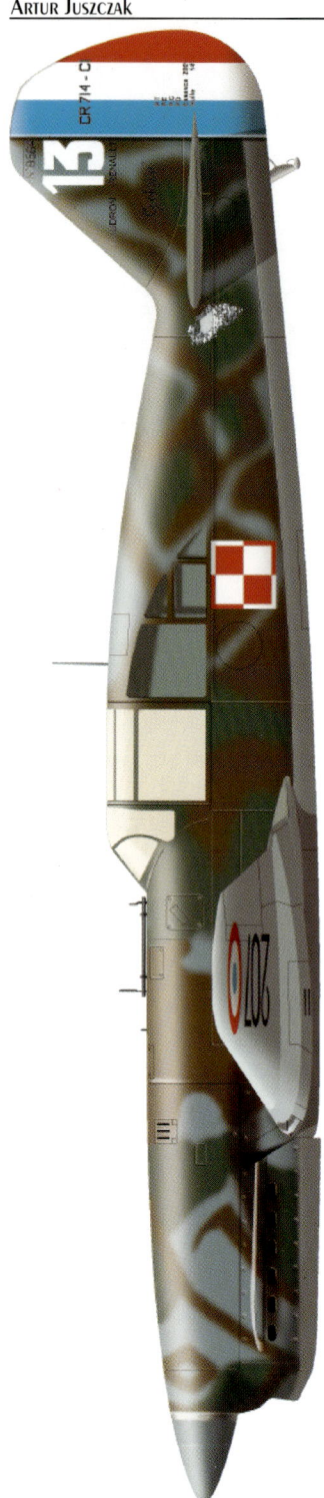

This and opposite page:
Caudron Cyclone C 714 of 1 Esc GC 1/145 serial no 85-49 (I-207) ppor. Aleksy Żukowski (Polish). May 1940 at Villacoublay.

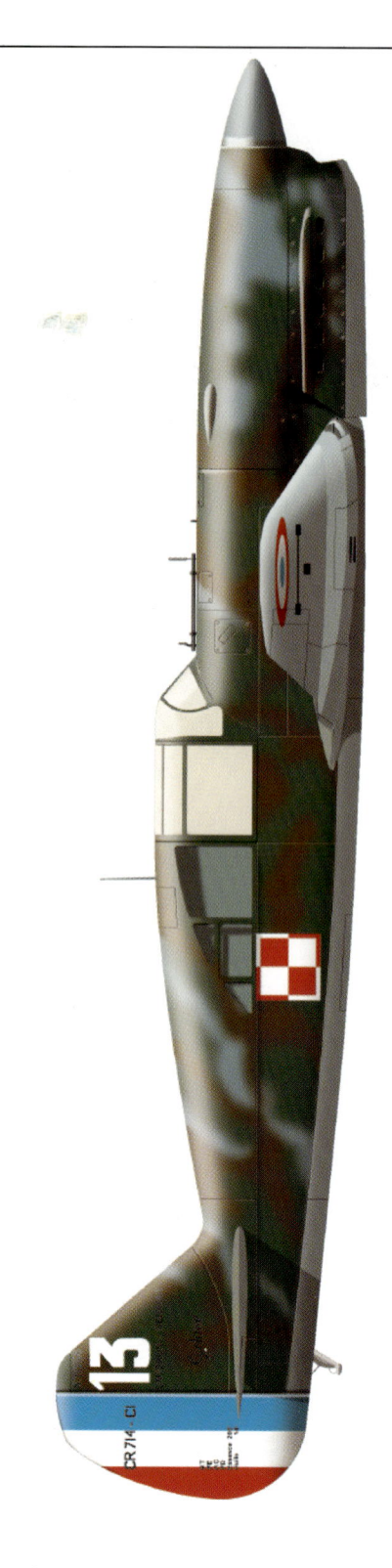

Colour Profiles

Fighters ... 151

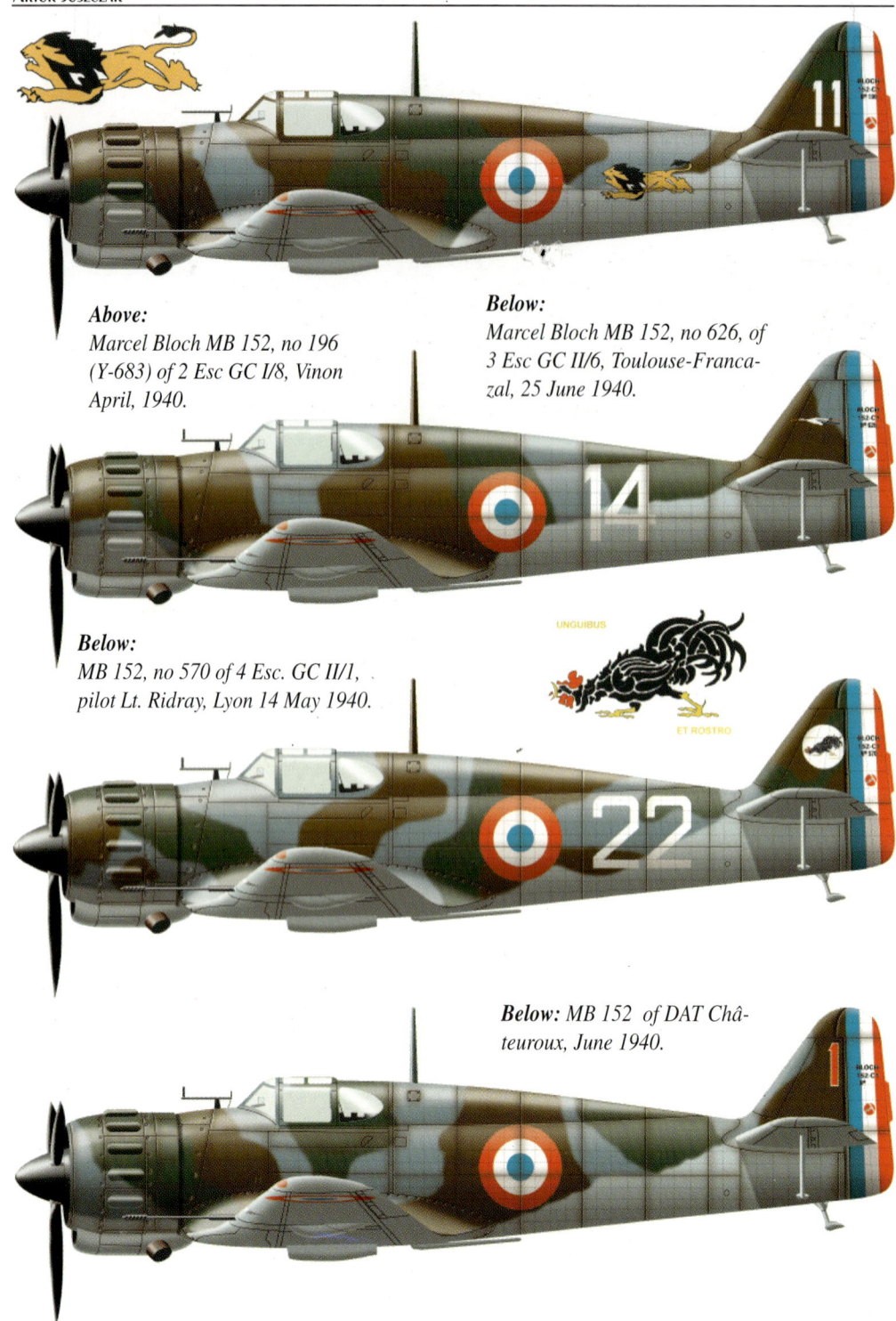

Above:
Marcel Bloch MB 152, no 196 (Y-683) of 2 Esc GC I/8, Vinon April, 1940.

Below:
Marcel Bloch MB 152, no 626, of 3 Esc GC II/6, Toulouse-Francazal, 25 June 1940.

Below:
MB 152, no 570 of 4 Esc. GC II/1, pilot Lt. Ridray, Lyon 14 May 1940.

Below: *MB 152 of DAT Châteuroux, June 1940.*